more than
less than

90 DEVOTIONS FOR DISCOVERING
YOUR INFINITE VALUE IN CHRIST

more than
less than

AMY DRUHOT

Copyright © 2025 by Amy Druhot
All rights reserved.

No part of this publication may be reproduced, stored in a retrieval system, or transmitted in any form or by any means — electronic, mechanical, photocopying, recording, or otherwise — without prior written permission of the publisher, except in the case of brief quotations embodied in critical articles or reviews.

Scripture References:
Unless otherwise noted, Scripture quotations are taken from the Holy Bible, *New International Version*®, NIV®.
Copyright © 1973, 1978, 1984, 2011 by Biblica, Inc.™
Used with permission. All rights reserved worldwide.

Additional translations (only list if used):
– NKJV: Scripture taken from the New King James Version®. Copyright © 1982 by Thomas Nelson. Used by permission. All rights reserved.
– ESV: Scripture quotations taken from *The Holy Bible, English Standard Version*®. Copyright © 2001 by Crossway. Used by permission. All rights reserved.

Edited by: Nancy Bach
Cover Design: Beling, 99Designs
Interior Layout: Six Penny Graphics

ISBN: 979-8-9902131-3-2
Printed in the United States of America

Publisher:
Just Brave It, LLC- JBI Publishing
Midlothian, Virginia

Disclaimer:
This devotional is not intended to provide professional counseling, medical, or psychological advice. The stories and reflections shared are based on the personal experiences of the author.

Ordering & Permissions:
For bulk orders, speaking inquiries, or permission requests, email:
amyd@justbraveit.com
or visit **www.justbraveit.com**

Mom,
Thank you for teaching me that in loving
Him most I could love others better.

Contents

Introduction xi

HIS LOVE

His Love 3

DAY 1:	Already Loved	5
DAY 2:	Still Chosen	7
DAY 3:	Lavished	9
DAY 4:	The Love That Fills Every Gap	11
DAY 5:	Wonderfully Made	13
DAY 6:	The God Who Sings	15
DAY 7:	Engraved	17
DAY 8:	Unbreakable	19
DAY 9:	The One Who Leaves the Ninety-Nine	21
DAY 10:	Unshaken Love	23
DAY 11:	Followed by Goodness	25
DAY 12:	Everlasting Love	27
DAY 13:	Love That Never Fails	29
DAY 14:	Greater Love	32
DAY 15:	The Kindness and Love of God	34
DAY 16:	Because of His Great Love	36
DAY 17:	The Son Who Loved Me	38
DAY 18:	Your Love Reaches the Heavens	40
DAY 19:	Who Is a God Like You?	42
DAY 20:	This Is Love	44

DAY 21: Loved First 46
DAY 22: Abounding in Love 48
DAY 23: Love Covers 50
DAY 24: Never Out of His Reach 52
DAY 25: Perfect Love Casts Out Fear 55
DAY 26: Above All 57
DAY 27: New Every Morning 59
DAY 28: Love That Covers 61
DAY 29: Love That Pursues 63
DAY 30: Love That Holds 65

HIS PLAN

His Plan 69

DAY 31: Plans That Prosper 71
DAY 32: Called for More 73
DAY 33: Divine Detours (My Burning Bush Moment) 76
DAY 34: The Waiting Room 79
DAY 35: The God Who Orders Steps 81
DAY 36: From Chaos to Clarity 83
DAY 37: Kingdom Timing 85
DAY 38: Surrendered Plans 87
DAY 39: Obedience Over Outcome 89
DAY 40: The Potter's Hands 92
DAY 41: His Plan: The Body He Built for Purpose 94
DAY 42: You Matter Here 96
DAY 43: Calling Ground 98
DAY 44: There's a Plan for You, Too 101

DAY 45: Listening for the Whisper 104
DAY 46: Bloom Where You're Planted 106
DAY 47: The Shepherd's Voice 109
DAY 48: When You Feel Behind 111
DAY 49: Ministry Without a Microphone 113
DAY 50: Divine Appointments 116
DAY 51: Clearing the Clutter 119
DAY 52: Out With the Old 121
DAY 53: Unfinished and Unforgotten 123
DAY 54: The Worthy Work 125
DAY 55: Hearing His Direction 127
DAY 56: Purpose in the Pain 129
DAY 57: The Refining Fire 131
DAY 58: The Divine Cleanup Crew 133
DAY 59: The Worth of His Plan 135
DAY 60: The Promise in the Plan 137

HIS PROMISE

His Promise 143

DAY 61: Standing on His Word 145
DAY 62: Unshakable Hope 147
DAY 63: The Peace Promise 149
DAY 64: Provision in Every Season 151
DAY 65: Never Alone 153
DAY 66: Beauty from Ashes 155
DAY 67: Strength Renewed 157
DAY 68: The Promise Keeper 159

DAY 69:	The Gift of Grace	161
DAY 70:	Faith Over Fear	163
DAY 71:	Joy Comes in the Morning	165
DAY 72:	Guarded by Peace	167
DAY 73:	Firm Foundation	169
DAY 74:	Redeemed and Restored	171
DAY 75:	His Promise: Redeemed Confidence	173
DAY 76:	Light in the Darkness	176
DAY 77:	Eternal Perspective	178
DAY 78:	He Fights for You	180
DAY 79:	Chosen and Kept	182
DAY 80:	The Crown of Life	184
DAY 81:	The Promise of People	186
DAY 82:	The Promise of Renewal	188
DAY 83:	Overflow	190
DAY 84:	Unmovable Confidence	192
DAY 85:	The Promise of Rest	194
DAY 86:	The Promise of Freedom	196
DAY 87:	The Promise of Purpose in Every Season	198
DAY 88:	His Promise, Your Peace	200
DAY 89:	The Promise of Forever Love	202
DAY 90:	The Promise of Forever	204

To The Extraordinary Woman Reading This:	207
Acknowledgments	210
About the Author	213

DAY 45: Listening for the Whisper 104
DAY 46: Bloom Where You're Planted 106
DAY 47: The Shepherd's Voice 109
DAY 48: When You Feel Behind 111
DAY 49: Ministry Without a Microphone 113
DAY 50: Divine Appointments 116
DAY 51: Clearing the Clutter 119
DAY 52: Out With the Old 121
DAY 53: Unfinished and Unforgotten 123
DAY 54: The Worthy Work 125
DAY 55: Hearing His Direction 127
DAY 56: Purpose in the Pain 129
DAY 57: The Refining Fire 131
DAY 58: The Divine Cleanup Crew 133
DAY 59: The Worth of His Plan 135
DAY 60: The Promise in the Plan 137

HIS PROMISE

His Promise 143

DAY 61: Standing on His Word 145
DAY 62: Unshakable Hope 147
DAY 63: The Peace Promise 149
DAY 64: Provision in Every Season 151
DAY 65: Never Alone 153
DAY 66: Beauty from Ashes 155
DAY 67: Strength Renewed 157
DAY 68: The Promise Keeper 159

DAY 69:	The Gift of Grace	161
DAY 70:	Faith Over Fear	163
DAY 71:	Joy Comes in the Morning	165
DAY 72:	Guarded by Peace	167
DAY 73:	Firm Foundation	169
DAY 74:	Redeemed and Restored	171
DAY 75:	His Promise: Redeemed Confidence	173
DAY 76:	Light in the Darkness	176
DAY 77:	Eternal Perspective	178
DAY 78:	He Fights for You	180
DAY 79:	Chosen and Kept	182
DAY 80:	The Crown of Life	184
DAY 81:	The Promise of People	186
DAY 82:	The Promise of Renewal	188
DAY 83:	Overflow	190
DAY 84:	Unmovable Confidence	192
DAY 85:	The Promise of Rest	194
DAY 86:	The Promise of Freedom	196
DAY 87:	The Promise of Purpose in Every Season	198
DAY 88:	His Promise, Your Peace	200
DAY 89:	The Promise of Forever Love	202
DAY 90:	The Promise of Forever	204

To The Extraordinary Woman Reading This:	207
Acknowledgments	210
About the Author	213

Introduction

If you've ever looked in the mirror and thought, *"I'm not enough,"* or *"I should be further along by now,"* or *"Why does she have it all together while I can barely find matching socks?"* well, friend, then you're exactly who this devotional is for.

I wrote this devotional for the women who are doing their best but still feel like they're somehow coming up short. The women who love Jesus but sometimes wonder if He might be a little disappointed in them. The women who are juggling a thousand titles—mom, wife, friend, leader, boss, volunteer, chaos manager—and yet somehow still feel like they're missing the one title that really matters: *worthy*.

This book is for you, because I *am* you.

When I first started writing, I didn't set out to write a devotional. Actually, I resisted it—*hard*. I had already written *Just Brave It*, which was filled with humor and grit and all the pep talks I wish someone had given me in the hardest chapters of my life. It was about courage, confidence, and choosing bravery over burnout. And it resonated. But as I kept speaking, meeting women, and sharing my story, I started to feel that gentle tug from God—you know, the one that starts as a whisper and eventually turns into a full-on shove?

That was me. Shoved into obedience.

God kept reminding me that the message He had given me through *Just Brave It* was never meant to stop at "be brave." It was meant to lead to *be still*. To trust. To surrender. To understand your worth not because of what you do, but because of who you are in Him.

And I'll be honest, I didn't want to write *this* book.

Because writing a faith-based devotional meant showing up differently. It meant laying my own spiritual journey bare. It meant admitting that I don't always get it right—that even though I can stand on a stage and talk about bravery, I still have days when I feel less than brave. Less than worthy. Less than enough.

But every time I tried to talk myself out of it, God whispered, "Not your plan, Amy—Mine."

So here we are.

This devotional—*More Than, Less Than: 90 Devotions for Discovering your Infinite Value in Christ*—is my surrender story. It's what happens when you finally stop running long enough to let God rewrite your formula for fulfillment.

See, a few years ago, I created what I called The Formula for Fulfillment:

Who + Why + How = Fulfillment

At the time, I thought it was just a clever motivational framework—something to help women align their identity, purpose, and action. But as I've grown (and as God has continued to patiently and persistently teach me), I've realized it was never *my* formula to begin with. It was His.

I just didn't know it yet.

Our *who* is not defined by the world—it's defined by Him and his deep love for us.

Our *why* is not our ambition—it's His plan.

Our *how* is not how brave we are in the hustle—it's His promise.

And when we align those pieces—His identity, His purpose, His power—we finally find what we've been chasing all along: peace. Fulfillment. The deep knowing that we are loved, chosen, and seen exactly as we are.

Now, that doesn't mean this process is easy. Spoiler alert: It's not.

I fought God on this book. I told Him I wasn't qualified, that I didn't have the perfect faith life, that maybe someone else could do it better. And you know what He said back? *"I know, that's why you're the one I want."*

Because if there's one thing I've learned about God, it's that He loves using imperfect people to show His perfect love.

You'll see that all throughout these pages. I don't write from the perspective of someone who's figured it all out—I write as someone who's been refined, stretched, humbled, and sometimes flat-out stubborn. (I'm what you might call a "burning bush kind of girl." God knows I'll need something on fire before I get the message.)

You'll laugh a little, probably cry once or twice, and, if I've done my job, you'll finish these 90 days with a heart that feels a little lighter, a little braver, and a lot more loved.

Every story in here points back to one simple truth: You are *more than* the labels, mistakes, and lies that make you feel *less than.*

You are *more than* what you do, what you have, or how the world measures your success.

You are *more than* the rejection, the missed opportunity, or the season that didn't go as planned.

And you are *infinitely more* than the enemy wants you to believe.

You are God's handiwork. His masterpiece. His favorite creation.

You were never meant to strive for worth—you were created from it.

So if you're tired of feeling like you're constantly auditioning for love or approval, I hope these pages remind you that you already have both. If you're walking through a season of waiting, confusion, or pressure, I hope you'll see the Potter's hands at work in your story. And if you're ready to rediscover your worth in Christ—well, sister, grab your coffee, open your Bible, and let's dig in.

Because you are *already loved, still chosen,* and *never less than enough.*

You ARE More Than Less Than.

Now, let's get brave about it.

HIS LOVE

His Love

Let's be real. "God loves you" has become the Christian version of "Have a nice day." We've heard it so many times it almost loses its punch, like a phrase you repeat until the words stop meaning anything. But when life gets heavy or confusing, that truth isn't cliché; it's oxygen. We just forget to breathe it in.

His *love isn't a concept; it's the context for your entire life.*

If you've ever struggled to feel enough—pretty enough, smart enough, strong enough, spiritual enough—this next 30 days is for you. Because before you can ever understand your *value* in Christ, you have to understand the *heart* of Christ.

His love isn't based on your performance; it's anchored in His promise. It doesn't show up when you've finally got it all together; it's what holds you together when everything feels like it's falling apart.

And maybe that's what makes His love so hard to grasp—it's not transactional; it's transformational. It doesn't just say, "I love you." It says, "I made you. I see you. I chose you. Still."

So for the next 30 days, we're going to peel back the layers of what the world says love is—conditional, earned, temporary—and sit in what His love actually means—*unchanging, unearned, and absolutely relentless.*

Because until you really know His love, you'll keep searching for your worth in places that were never meant to define it.

So take a deep breath. You don't have to prove anything here. You don't have to perform or polish yourself up. You just have to show up—right where you are.

Because *His love* isn't something you have to chase.

It's something you get to receive.

And once you do ... everything about how you see yourself will start to change.

DAY 1

Already Loved

> "For God so loved the world that He gave His one and only Son, that whoever believes in Him shall not perish but have eternal life." — *John 3:16*

I know, I know—we're starting with the most obvious verse in the Bible. You've seen it on bumper stickers, coffee mugs, T-shirts, maybe even a football player's eye black. But hang with me for a second, because I think sometimes the verses we know best are the ones we stop actually hearing.

Have you ever felt unlovable? Or maybe you've loved deeply and had that love taken away. Heartbreak—whether it's from a person, a friendship, a job, or even our own self-disappointment—is something we all experience. It's unavoidable.

We're wired to crave love. And if we're honest, most of us have spent at least a season of life treating love like a scoreboard—measuring our worth by who gives it, who withholds it, and how long it lasts.

But here's the truth tucked inside this famous verse: For God so loved you ...

Not just the world—you.

God's love isn't measured in performance or popularity. It's not given when we're doing everything right and taken back when we stumble. Human love can be conditional. It can fade, shift, or disappoint. But God's love, the kind described here, never wavers.

The word "world" is intentional. He could've said, "For God so loved the good people," or "the ones who go to church every Sunday," or "the ones who never lose their temper in traffic." But no. He said world—meaning everyone. All of us. The whole imperfect, chaotic, trying-our-best-but-still-messing-up world.

And that includes you.

The truth is, there's nothing you can do to make Him love you more, and nothing you can do to make Him love you less. His love isn't earned; it's given. It's not a reward—it's a promise.

And here's the part that gets me every time: Even if you don't believe in Him, He still loves you. You were already loved before you ever took your first breath, before your first heartbreak, before your first mistake.

So, the next time you start to measure your worth by how someone else treats you, stop and remember this: You are already fully loved by the One who doesn't change His mind about you.

That's the love to anchor your value in—the love that never fails, never fades, and never leaves. You are loved. Always have been. Always will be.

Prayer:

Lord, thank You for loving me long before I ever tried to earn it. Help me to stop chasing validation that can't compare to the love You've already given me. When I start to forget my worth or measure it by the world's standards, remind me that I am Yours—fully, completely, and forever loved. Teach me to rest in that truth today.
Amen.

DAY 2

Still Chosen

> "But God demonstrates His own love for us in this: While we were still sinners, Christ died for us." — *Romans 5:8*

I have a confession: I am about the most human human there ever was. I may not be great at a lot of things, but what I am really good at? Sin. Not on purpose—I don't wake up thinking, "How can I disappoint Jesus today?" But just by being human, I've gotten really good at the messy stuff. Sometimes it feels like no matter how hard I try to do right, I still manage to trip over my own good intentions on the way there.

Maybe you've been there too—trying your best to live right, love people well, and stay on track … and then boom. You lose your temper, speak too soon, act out of fear, or make a bad decision and find yourself saying, "Welp, there goes my halo."

I've loved Jesus my whole life. But even with that love, there have been plenty of moments when I've looked up at heaven and said, "Okay, Jesus, I know this is wrong … but I'm gonna need You to just walk with me through it, okay?" (Yes, those were my actual words. Don't judge—He's heard worse.)

Now mix all that with my Type A perfectionist tendencies and you've got yourself a Christian hot mess express. I've spent years trying to be perfect—for God, for people, for myself—and still found myself tripping over my own humanity every single time. My "human" tends to show, and not always in the most flattering ways.

So, when God started tugging on my heart about ministry a few years ago, my first instinct was to run. And listen, I love a good workout, but this was what I would refer to as avoidance cardio. Because how could God use someone who still messes up, doubts herself, and sometimes forgets to pray before reacting?

Here's what I learned though—you can't outrun God or His purpose for your life.

And here's the even better part. He doesn't need your perfection to use you; He just wants your willingness.

God loves you exactly as you are, not as you think you should be by now. He sees your broken pieces and still says, "I can work with that." In fact, it's often those very cracks—the ones we try so hard to hide—that let His light shine through the brightest.

My ministry with women isn't built on having it all figured out; it's built on knowing I don't—and realizing that His love still covers me anyway. That's what Romans 5:8 is all about. While we were still sinners—before we fixed the mess, before we even tried—Christ died for us.

That's not the love of a God waiting for you to get it together. That's the love of a God who steps right into the middle of your chaos, grabs your hand, and says, "I'm not leaving."

So, if you're feeling a little too human today, take a breath. You're not the exception—you're the reason for grace. You're still chosen. Still loved. Still His.

Prayer:

Lord, thank You for loving me even when I'm a hot mess. Thank You for reminding me that Your love isn't about my perfection; it's about Your grace. Help me to stop running from my purpose and start resting in the truth that You can use me—exactly as I am. Amen.

DAY 3

Lavished

> "See what great love the Father has lavished on us, that we should be called children of God! And that is what we are." — *1 John 3:1*

Have you ever wanted to be liked so badly that you bent yourself into someone else's shape just to fit? Yeah, girl, me too.

I give love in a big way—I always have. It's just who I am. But here's the thing I've learned the hard way: Not everyone is going to receive that love the same way I give it. And if you're anything like me, that can be a tough pill to swallow.

For years, I chased validation like it was my full-time job—desperately wanting to be liked, accepted, understood. I wanted everyone to see my heart and think, *"Ooh, I like her."* But life doesn't work that way, does it? The more I tried to earn approval, the emptier I felt.

When I wrote my first book, *Just Brave It*, I poured out the most personal, tender parts of my story. I honestly believed that if I let people see the real me—the brave, the broken, the learning—it would make them feel more comfortable with their own story too. And while that did happen for many, I also learned something else: Not everyone will celebrate your courage.

Some people will misunderstand you. Some will judge you. And some just … won't like you. Sometimes for a reason, sometimes for no reason at all. When you step out and live in your purpose, you're not just putting your gifts out there—you're putting *yourself* out there. And that means being seen not just for your beauty, but for your flaws.

I had to learn to stop measuring my worth by other people's reactions. Their acceptance isn't my assignment. Their approval isn't my identity.

Here's the truth I had to come back to—and maybe you need to as well: God's love isn't something you earn. It's something He *lavishes*. That word means extravagant, overflowing, abundant—the kind of love that doesn't make sense but never runs out.

He loves you when you're brave, and He loves you when you're hiding. He loves you when you get it right, and He loves you when you fall flat on your face.

Not to brag, but He's pretty obsessed with me. But also ... with you.

So, when the world feels loud and your heart feels bruised from trying to belong, remember this: You already belong to Him. You're not waiting to be chosen—you *are* chosen. You're not fighting for love—you *are* loved. Fully. Lavishly. Unconditionally.

Wrap yourself in that kind of love today. Let it be the one opinion that defines you.

Prayer:

Father, thank You for loving me with a love that doesn't depend on how well I perform or how many people approve of me. Help me rest in the truth that I am already accepted, already chosen, already Yours. Teach me to stop seeking the world's validation and start living from the fullness of Your love. Amen.

DAY 4

The Love That Fills Every Gap

> "And may you have the power to understand, as all God's people should, how wide, how long, how high, and how deep His love is. May you experience the love of Christ, though it is too great to understand fully." — *Ephesians 3:18–19*

I always wanted to be a mother. My mom was really good at her career as a stay-at-home mom—and I mean really good. She poured more meaning and intention into that role than most CEOs I've worked with over the years. So, little me was inspired by the best kind of role model. I had my plan: good wife, white picket fence, two or three cute kids, and a perfect front-porch Christmas card photo every December.

That was the dream.

Then cue 20-year-old Amy—no husband, still living at home, and pregnant. Let's just say that Christmas card didn't exactly fit the original vision.

I needed Jesus more than ever. So, I went to the one place I thought I'd find Him: church. But instead of being greeted by His love, I was greeted by stares and whispers. I felt so ashamed. Embarrassed. Alone. I can still remember the weight of that moment—the way my chest felt tight, my eyes stayed low, and I just wanted to disappear.

Here's the truth: We're all human. Even in church. And humans judge. I'm not upset at those women for that—I've done the same thing a time or two in my own ways. But in that season, I didn't need judgment. I needed grace. I didn't need to be reminded of my mistakes; I needed to be reminded of His mercy.

I thought I had to go to church to find Jesus. But what I learned is that He was never limited to a building. Even when I felt far from Him, He wasn't far from me. He wasn't shocked by my story. He wasn't surprised by how I got there. He was with me—in it—loving me through it all.

That's the beauty of God's love. It fills every gap—the ones between who we are and who we hoped we'd be, between shame and forgiveness, between our mistakes and His mercy. His love is wider than your worst day, deeper than your disappointment, and higher than any judgment the world can throw your way.

If you've ever felt too far gone, too flawed, or too unworthy, hear me: You're not. You were never out of His reach. You don't have to clean up to come close—He's already in the middle of your mess, arms wide open.

His love doesn't avoid your story; it steps right into it. And it fills every gap.

Prayer:

Lord, thank You for meeting me right in the middle of my story. Thank You for loving me when I felt unworthy, unseen, or too far gone. Help me remember that Your love fills every space my shame tries to occupy. Teach me to rest in that truth—that nothing, not even my past, can separate me from You. Amen.

DAY 5

Wonderfully Made

> "For you created my inmost being; you knit me together in my mother's womb. I praise you because I am fearfully and wonderfully made; your works are wonderful; I know that full well." — *Psalm 139:13–14*

Let's be real—some days the mirror feels like an enemy. The lighting's bad, your jeans are rude, and the woman staring back at you looks more like "tired Amazon return" than "fearfully and wonderfully made."

And if I'm being honest, my struggle with feeling *less than* hasn't just been just about measuring up on the inside—it's been in that reflection too.

The things I've said to myself, both out loud and in my head, I wouldn't say to my worst enemy. *Why are we so cruel to ourselves?* We would never talk to our best friend that way, but somehow, we've decided it's fair game when it's our own reflection looking back.

For years, I picked myself apart—the body that's carried me through every season, the face that tells the story of both laughter and tears, the woman who's done her best to show up even when it was hard. I talked down to her, doubted her, and dismissed her as "not enough."

But God ... He's never seen me that way.

When I look in the mirror and see flaws, He sees *features*. When

I see failure, He sees *form and function*. He looks at me, and at you, and says, "That one's Mine."

We scroll through flawless feeds and forget that the same God who painted sunsets and scattered stars also handcrafted us—freckles, scars, dimples, and all. He didn't make a mistake.

I used to think loving myself was vain. Now I know it's *holy*. Because when I reject what He made, I'm not being humble—I'm disagreeing with the Creator of the universe.

So here's your reminder, sister: God didn't make you to be a "before photo." You are His living, breathing, work-in-progress masterpiece—messy bun, stretch marks, and all.

When He looks at you, He doesn't see lack; He sees love.

Prayer:

Lord, thank You for crafting me with such care and intention. Help me to silence the voice of comparison and cruelty in my own mind. When I'm tempted to tear myself down, remind me that I am Your creation—fearfully, wonderfully, and purposefully made. Let my reflection remind me of Your love, not my flaws. Amen.

DAY 6

The God Who Sings

> "The Lord your God is with you, the Mighty Warrior who saves. He will take great delight in you; in His love He will no longer rebuke you, but will rejoice over you with singing." — *Zephaniah 3:17*

==He doesn't just love you==—He *likes* you. Enough to sing over you.

If God has a playlist, your name is on it.

One day I was driving, listening to "How Long Will I Love You"—the Ellie Goulding version—when mid-song I heard something I swear wasn't there before. The lyrics in my head shifted, just slightly, as if God Himself were whispering through them:

"How long will I give to you? As long as I live through you."

I had to start the song over and listen again. And again. My eyes filled with tears because it didn't just *sound* like a love song anymore—it **felt** like one. A serenade from God straight to my heart. A reminder that His love isn't distant or formal; it's personal, intimate, and full of joy.

That's how much He loves us. He doesn't just love us because He has to—He delights in us because He *wants to*. He's not the disappointed parent tapping His foot waiting for us to get it right. He's the Father who smiles when we show up, the one who celebrates our return, the one who sings over us even when we're still figuring it out.

Sometimes I think we imagine God's face as serious, maybe

even frustrated—like He's keeping score of all the times we missed the mark. But Zephaniah 3:17 paints a completely different picture. God is *filled with joy* when you walk with Him. He's so full of love for you that it spills out in song.

If you've ever been serenaded or slow-danced or simply felt seen in a love that takes your breath away—that's a glimpse of how God feels about you. Not the cleaned-up, church-ready version of you, but the real, honest, trying-your-best version.

He rejoices over *you*. Every single day.

Not just when you're strong—but when you're struggling.

Not just when you're winning—but when you're weary.

His melody doesn't change with your mood. His song stays the same: one of delight, devotion, and unshakable love.

So, the next time you find yourself wondering if you've disappointed Him, try to imagine Him humming your name instead—smiling, singing, completely smitten that you're His.

Prayer:

Lord, thank You for loving me with a joy so deep it overflows into song. Help me to hear Your melody louder than the noise of self-doubt or shame. Remind me that You don't just love me—You delight in me. Teach me to live today knowing I am Your favorite song. Amen.

DAY 7

Engraved

> "See, I have engraved you on the palms of my hands; your walls are ever before me." — *Isaiah 49:16*

I was always taught that my body is a temple. And in a lot of Christian circles, that usually means one thing ... *no tattoos.*

Now, remember earlier when I said I'm really good at the messy part of life? Did I also mention I have a tattoo? And because I grew up in the late '90s, you can probably guess where it is.

Yep. I'm part of the *lower back tattoo crew.*

Let's just say it wasn't my parents' proudest moment. The discovery happened one Thanksgiving when I leaned over to put something in the oven, and there it was—the family dinner showstopper no one asked for. (*Oh, how I wish high waist mom jeans had been in style then!*)

Not exactly my most "holy temple" moment.

But here's what I've come to love about this verse in Isaiah. God says, *"I have engraved you on the palms of My hands."* Engraved. Not written in pencil. Not stamped in temporary ink. Engraved—permanent, intentional, unerasable.

When I think about that, I can't help but laugh a little. Because while my tattoo might fade over time (and probably wasn't my best decision-making moment), the mark God has on me never will. His "tattoo" is eternal.

You see, that's what His love does—it marks you as His. You are literally carved into His hands, held in His care, remembered every moment. He doesn't hide His marks, either. They're proof of His love—the same hands that were pierced for you now hold your name forever.

And unlike my Thanksgiving tattoo reveal, He's never ashamed of the mark He carries. He's proud of it. Proud of *you*.

We spend so much of our lives worrying about our scars, our mistakes, or the parts of our story we wish we could cover up. But God sees those same parts and says, "That's my girl. She's mine."

The world might call it a flaw. He calls it evidence of grace.

So, whether your "mark" is a literal tattoo, a scar, a past mistake, or something you're still healing from—remember this: God has written your name into His story with love that cannot fade. You're not penciled in. You're *engraved*.

Prayer:

Lord, thank You for engraving my name on Your hands and calling me Yours forever. Help me to stop hiding the parts of my story that You've already redeemed. Thank You for seeing beauty where I see regret, and for loving me so deeply that You've made me a permanent part of You. Amen.

DAY 8

Unbreakable

> "For I am convinced that neither death nor life, neither angels nor demons, neither the present nor the future, nor any powers, neither height nor depth, nor anything else in all creation, will be able to separate us from the love of God that is in Christ Jesus our Lord." — *Romans 8:38–39*

Imagine this: Someone you look up to and respect comes to you and offers the opportunity of a lifetime. They've thought of every detail, mapped out every step, and all you have to do is show up and trust them. The plan is good—better than anything you could come up with yourself—and yet ... you refuse. Not just refuse, but ignore, hide, and run.

That's been my life for the past few years.

God's direction for me wasn't vague. It wasn't subtle. I'm talking clear-as-day, tugging-on-my-heart, burning-bush-level moments. (And don't worry—we'll get to my burning bush metaphor later.) It was as if God Himself had handed me the map, highlighted the path, and said, "Amy, this is what I created you for."

And I still chose fear over faith.

Over and over again.

And all while speaking to women across the nation about bravery—oh, the irony!

If you've ever done the same—felt God calling you toward something and responded with a nervous laugh and a "Maybe later, Lord"—I want you to know you're not alone. We all have moments when fear gets loud, when the unknown feels safer to avoid than to face.

But here's what amazes me about God: Even when I've run, doubted, hesitated, or flat-out resisted, His love hasn't budged an inch. I can't outrun it, out-sin it, or outsmart it. It's unbreakable.

Romans 8:38–39 says there is *nothing* that can separate us from His love. Not fear. Not failure. Not our avoidance. Not our pretending to be brave while quietly falling apart. His love is steady—constant when I'm inconsistent, faithful when I'm hesitant, patient when I'm stubborn.

Sometimes I picture it like this: me, running in circles, clutching my plans, while God stands calmly in the middle of my chaos—hand extended, heart open, saying, "I'll wait. I'm not going anywhere."

And He doesn't.

That's the kind of love we can't fully comprehend—the love that doesn't pull away when we do, the love that chases us down when we'd rather hide, the love that refuses to let go no matter how many times we choose fear over faith.

So, if you're in a season where you've been running from what God's calling you to do—slow down. Turn around. His love hasn't gone anywhere. It never does.

He's still there. Still waiting. Still loving you. Unbreakably.

Prayer:

Lord, thank You for loving me through every moment I've doubted, resisted, or run from what You've called me to. Thank You that Your love is steady when I'm not. Give me the courage to choose faith over fear, to trust Your plan, and to rest in the truth that Your love will never let me go. Amen.

DAY 9

The One Who Leaves the Ninety-Nine

> *"Suppose one of you has a hundred sheep and loses one of them. Doesn't he leave the ninety-nine in the open country and go after the lost sheep until he finds it?" — Luke 15:3–7*

If you're in my friend circle, you've probably heard me say, *"I'm what you'd call a burning-bush kinda girl. I'd like to be a mustard seed, but no—I need a bush on fire."*

But it wasn't always that way.

Little Amy had mustard-seed faith—the kind that doesn't flinch. Her heart was steady, simple, certain that God was good and always near. But somewhere between childhood and adulthood, life started handing me questions. I didn't stop believing, but I did start wrestling. I wanted to understand not just *what* I believed but *why*.

And somewhere in that process, my faith grew quiet. Months without prayer. Days when thoughts of God barely crossed my mind. I wasn't angry at Him—I was just busy, distracted, running on empty. Getting by instead of growing.

And yet ... every time I found my way back, He was there. Arms-wide-open kind of love.

That's who He is—the Shepherd who notices when one sheep wanders off and refuses to leave her behind.

When I picture the parable of the lost sheep, I imagine the

Shepherd scanning the hillside, counting heads, realizing—someone's missing. Then He drops everything and goes after her. Through the brush, through the dark, through the danger—until He finds her.

That's me. That's you.

We're the ones who wander, question, overthink, or quietly drift—and yet He never stops coming after us. His love isn't passive; it pursues.

Even in my seasons of silence, He was moving toward me. Even when my prayers were whispers, He heard them. Even when I needed a burning bush to remind me He was near, He showed up—not to scold me for getting lost, but to scoop me up, dust me off, and walk me home.

Maybe today you feel like the one that got away. Maybe you've been distracted, distant, or unsure of how to find your way back. The good news? You don't have to. The Shepherd is already on His way.

He always comes for His own—every time.

Prayer:
Lord, thank You for being the kind of Shepherd who never gives up on me. Thank You for seeking me out when I wander and for loving me enough to chase me down. When my faith grows quiet, remind me that Your footsteps are already coming my way. Amen.

DAY 10

Unshaken Love

> "'Though the mountains be shaken and the hills be removed, yet my unfailing love for you will not be shaken nor my covenant of peace be removed,' says the Lord, who has compassion on you." — Isaiah 54:10

In my book *Just Brave It,* I shared what I call *The Formula for Fulfillment*—the same framework I later built my TEDx talk around. It's simple, but it changed everything for me. The first part of that formula starts with understanding your "Who."

When I was writing it, I realized how often we, especially as women, find our identity in what we *do* instead of who we *are*. We tie our worth to the titles we carry—mother, wife, VP of sales, author, speaker—and to the applause that sometimes comes with them.

And let's be honest—those titles can bring joy and purpose. They can fill our hearts and make us feel seen and significant. But the danger is this: When the titles shift or disappear, we can start to feel like we've disappeared too.

When the job changes …
When the babies grow up …
When the applause fades …
When the season ends …

We can suddenly feel lost—like we've misplaced who we are somewhere between everyone else's needs and expectations.

That's why this verse in Isaiah is so powerful. God says that even when the mountains move—when the most stable, permanent things in life start to shake—*His love does not.* His compassion, His peace, His purpose for you ... none of it changes.

You are loved and chosen not because of the title you hold but because of the name you bear—His.

And friend, that kind of love is steady. It's not based on your performance or productivity. It's not tied to your season or your success. It's the kind of love that sits with you when everything else falls apart and whispers, "You are still Mine."

If your world feels unsteady right now—if your identity feels uncertain because something you built your worth on has shifted—take heart. His love has not moved.

You are not the sum of your titles. You are the sum of His affection.

Unshaken. Unmoved. Unchanging.

Prayer:

Lord, thank You for loving me beyond my titles and accomplishments. Thank You that even when life shifts and my roles change, Your love for me stays the same. Help me root my identity in who You say I am, not what I do. Teach me to rest in the truth that Your love is the only thing that will never be shaken. Amen.

DAY 11

Followed by Goodness

> "Surely goodness and love will follow me
> all the days of my life." — *Psalm 23:6*

There are a lot of things these days that seem *too good to be true*.

Scroll social media for five minutes and you'll find them—the ads for the "next best thing." And your girl falls for them *every time*. Gold eye patches, teeth whiteners, lip plumpers, collagen face masks that go clear (because apparently opaque isn't enough to erase 10 years), my personal new favorite—the lymphatic drainage face brush—and so much "body lift cream" that by now, I should probably be hanging from the ceiling.

Now, whether those things actually work or not is … up for debate. But one thing that's not—is the goodness of God's love. It's the real deal. Works every time.

Psalm 23:6 reminds us that *goodness and love follow us all the days of our lives*. Not some of the days. Not just the good ones. *All* of them.

Here's what I love about that: God's goodness doesn't wait for us to get it all together—it follows us even when we wander. It's not chasing us down to scold us; it's there to shepherd us. To guide us back home.

There have been seasons in my life when I didn't see His goodness until I looked back. I thought I was on my own, trying to piece things together, when in reality, He was working behind the scenes the entire time—closing doors that needed to close, protecting me from things I didn't even know I needed protection from, and redirecting me toward something better.

That's how His goodness works. It's steady. Quiet sometimes, but constant. It doesn't expire when we doubt, and it doesn't fade when we fail.

We live in a world full of flashy promises—things that sparkle, shout, and say, "This will change your life!" But the truth is, most of them don't. God's love, though? It does. Every single time.

It doesn't wear off. It doesn't stop working. And you don't need a 10-step routine to access it. It's already following you ... right now, today, exactly where you are.

So, when you find yourself scrolling past all the "too good to be true" ads, let it remind you: There *is* something good that's always true. His love. His mercy. His relentless goodness—following you all the days of your life.

> *Prayer:*
> *Lord, thank You for Your goodness that never lets me go. Even when I don't see it, even when I wander, You're still right behind me—guiding, protecting, and loving me. Help me to recognize Your goodness today and trust that it's always at work in my life. Amen.*

DAY 12

Everlasting Love

> "The Lord appeared to us in the past, saying: 'I have loved you with an everlasting love; I have drawn you with unfailing kindness.'" — *Jeremiah 31:3*

Some things in life have an expiration date. Milk, mascara, relationships, jobs—even the "best by" label on a dream sometimes shows up sooner than we'd like. Seasons change. People drift. Circumstances shift.

But there's one thing that doesn't—God's love.

When Jeremiah wrote these words, God's people had messed up ... again. They'd run, wandered, and worn themselves out trying to find fulfillment everywhere else. And still, God said, *"I have loved you with an everlasting love."*

That word *everlasting* is wild if you really think about it. It means it's always been and will always be—before your first breath, through every chapter of your life, and long after the last page is written. His love isn't fragile or fleeting. It's not something you can lose, break, or outgrow.

If you're anything like me, you've probably gone through seasons where you wondered if you'd finally reached the limit of His patience. Times when you thought, "Surely, He's tired of rescuing me by now." But He's not. He's still there—arms open, heart steady, love unchanged.

When I look back at my own story, I see it so clearly—His kindness in the moments I didn't deserve it, His mercy when I couldn't see past my own mistakes, His quiet faithfulness holding everything together when I was falling apart. That's what everlasting love looks like: consistent in every season, unshaken by every storm.

Maybe right now you're in a season where love feels conditional—where people's approval depends on what you do, or who you are to them. Take heart. God's love isn't like that. It's not based on your performance, your perfection, or your progress. It's based on who He is.

And He is everlasting.

So when the world shifts, when people leave, when your plans crumble, remember this: Nothing that begins or ends can compare to a love that never will.

Prayer:

Lord, thank You for loving me with an everlasting love—one that never runs out and never gives up. When I start to measure love by how it feels in the moment, remind me that Yours is constant, unchanging, and forever. Teach me to rest in that kind of love today. Amen.

DAY 13

Love That Never Fails

> "Love is patient, love is kind. It does not envy, it does not boast, it is not proud. It does not dishonor others, it is not self-seeking, it is not easily angered, it keeps no record of wrongs. Love does not delight in evil but rejoices with the truth. It always protects, always trusts, always hopes, always perseveres. Love never fails." — *1 Corinthians 13:4–8*

When I was a little girl, I was in a church play called *The Bee-Attitudes*. I'll give you one guess who I was—the sweetest of them all—"Honey Bee." My solo was this very verse from 1 Corinthians 13. Picture tiny Amy in sparkly red heart antenna headband, yellow wings, singing about patience and kindness like I was auditioning for Broadway. I still remember every lyric. Even then, something about that verse stuck.

Love that is patient.
Love that is kind.
Love that never fails.

Back then, it sounded sweet as "Honey" and simple to do. But now, years later, I know just how hard it really is to live out.

We've all heard this verse—probably at a wedding, right? It's the "pretty verse" that looks good in cursive on a wooden sign from Hobby Lobby. But if you've ever tried to actually *live* it out, you know this kind of love isn't easy.

Love that's patient and kind? Sure, on a good day. But love that doesn't keep score, that always hopes, that never fails? That's next-level love—and honestly, it's not something we can pull off on our own.

I've had plenty of moments where my love has fallen short—where my patience expired, my kindness was selective, and my forgiveness came with an asterisk. Because human love, no matter how well-intentioned, has limits. It bends, it breaks, it gets tired.

But God's love? It doesn't. His love is the kind that never keeps a list of wrongs. It's not performative or conditional. It's not earned, bought, or traded. It just *is*.

When Paul wrote this passage, he wasn't describing the love we naturally give—he was describing the love that comes from God Himself. A love that never fails because it's rooted in someone who never changes.

And that love is what He pours into you.

When you feel unlovable, He's patient.

When you're harsh on yourself, He's kind.

When you mess up again, He's forgiving—not rolling His eyes, not walking away. Just loving, protecting, and reminding you that nothing you do can make Him stop.

We live in a world full of "love ifs." *I'll love you if you act right. If you look right. If you succeed. If you fit in.* But God's love says, "I love you, period." No ifs. No buts. No conditions.

That's what makes His love fail-proof—because it's not based on us; it's based on Him.

So today, when your patience wears thin or your love feels small, remember this: The same love that shaped a little "Honey Bee" in a sparkly antenna headband is the same love still shaping you today. Because His love—truly—never fails.

Prayer:
Lord, thank You for loving me with a love that never fails—one that is patient, kind, and endlessly forgiving. Help me to reflect that kind of love to others, even when it's hard. Fill the gaps where my love falls short with Yours. Amen.

DAY 14

Greater Love

> "Greater love has no one than this: to lay down one's life for one's friends." — *John 15:13*

There are few verses that stop me in my tracks like this one does.

It's simple, but it carries a weight that can't be rushed past. "Greater love has no one than this." It's not about warm feelings or pretty words—it's about sacrifice. About love that gives everything.

Jesus spoke these words the night before He would live them out—when the cross was already in view. He wasn't talking in metaphors or parables. He was making a promise. He was saying, *This is what love really looks like.*

Love that lays itself down.

Love that steps forward when it would be easier to step back.

Love that chooses pain for the sake of redemption.

We throw the word "love" around easily—and maybe that's why it's easy to forget how fierce it really is. True love isn't soft or passive. It's active. It's brave. It's costly.

And that's the love we're invited into.

Not a love that demands perfection. Not a love that gives to get. But a love that reflects His—willing to sacrifice comfort, pride, control, or convenience for the sake of someone else.

When Jesus laid down His life, He wasn't just proving His love; He was defining it. He was showing us that love isn't measured in words, but in what we're willing to give for another.

This verse has always humbled me, because it reminds me that I didn't earn that kind of love—I just get to live in it. And when I think about how often I fall short of that standard, I'm overwhelmed all over again by His grace.

He didn't just die for His friends. He died for the ones who doubted Him. The ones who ran. The ones like me and you—who still stumble, still question, still forget.

And He calls that love *greater*.

If you ever find yourself wondering if you're worth it—if you've done too much, failed too often, or fallen too far—remember this verse. The answer has already been given, and it was written in blood: *You are.*

Prayer:

Jesus, thank You for showing me what real love looks like. Thank You for laying down Your life so I could live in freedom. Teach me to love with courage—not just in words, but in action. Help me remember that Your sacrifice wasn't just for the world, but for me. Amen.

DAY 15

The Kindness and Love of God

> "But when the kindness and love of God our Savior appeared, He saved us, not because of righteous things we had done, but because of His mercy." — *Titus 3:4–5*

Some people just get it. They have that rare, quiet superpower of showing up—not for attention, not for recognition, but because loving people well is just who they are.

My friend Noelle is one of those people.

This woman has the spiritual gift of *presence*. No matter how much she has going on in her own world—and believe me, she's had some heavy stuff—she still shows up for others with her whole heart. She's the friend who will drive hours just to surprise me at a book signing. The one who champions every crazy idea I have, who picks up the phone every single time I call (even when it's one of my 20-minute "just a quick thought" calls).

And it's not just me. I've watched her do it for others—again and again—without fanfare, without complaint, without keeping score.

That's the kind of love that reminds me of Jesus.

When Paul wrote to Titus, he described how *the kindness and love of God appeared*. Not in a sermon, not in a miracle, not even in a moment of judgment—but in *mercy*. In showing up. In meeting us right where we were, not because we earned it, but because that's who He is.

Noelle reminds me of that kind of love. She doesn't just say, "Let me know if you need anything." She *shows up*. She listens. She encourages. She reminds me—without ever saying the words—that love doesn't have to be loud to be powerful.

And that's what Jesus does for us. He shows up. Every time.

Even when we're not at our best.

Even when we're a mess.

Even when we've convinced ourselves we don't deserve it.

He keeps coming—with mercy, with grace, with kindness that doesn't make sense but changes everything.

So today, maybe ask yourself—who's been a "Noelle" in your life? And where might God be nudging you to be that person for someone else? Because the most beautiful way we reflect the love of God is when we choose to simply show up.

Prayer:

Lord, thank You for Your kindness—for showing up in my life again and again with grace and mercy I don't deserve. Thank You for friends like Noelle who reflect Your heart so beautifully. Help me to be that kind of love for others—the kind that shows up, stays present, and reminds people of You. Amen.

DAY 16

Because of His Great Love

> "But because of His great love for us, God, who is rich in mercy, made us alive with Christ even when we were dead in transgression—it is by grace you have been saved." —*Ephesians 2:4–5*

==There's something about those words==—because of His great love.

Not "because you got it together."

Not "because you followed all the rules."

Not even "because you finally learned your lesson."

Nope. Just because of His great love.

That's it. That's the reason for everything good in our story.

I've had plenty of moments in my life when I've felt spiritually flatlined—not gone, just ... going through the motions. Ever been there? You're alive, but not really living. You pray, but the words feel stale. You believe, but your heart feels numb. You love God, but you're running on fumes.

And yet—even in those moments—He breathes life back into us. Not because we deserve it, but because He refuses to let us stay lifeless.

This verse says that even when we were dead in our sin, He made us alive. That means His love doesn't wait for our pulse to return—it is the pulse. It's what brings us back.

There have been times when I've looked at my own heart and thought, *You should be further along by now.* Times when my faith felt small, my joy dim, and my motivation buried under exhaustion or doubt. But the beautiful, frustrating, humbling truth is that I can't earn my way back to life—only His love can do that.

Because of His great love, you are not too far gone.

Because of His great love, your story still matters.

Because of His great love, there's breath in your spiritual lungs today.

You don't have to perform your way into His grace—you just have to receive it.

So, if you're in a season where your faith feels flat or your spirit feels tired, let this be your reminder: You don't have to fix it all. You just have to open your hands and let His love do what it does best—bring you back to life.

Prayer:

Lord, thank You for loving me even when I feel lifeless inside. Thank You for meeting me in the quiet, tired spaces of my heart and breathing new life into me. Help me to stop striving and simply rest in Your great love—the love that makes me whole, alive, and free. Amen.

DAY 17

The Son Who Loved Me

> "I have been crucified with Christ and I no longer live, but Christ lives in me. The life I now live in the body, I live by faith in the Son of God, who loved me and gave Himself for me." — *Galatians 2:20*

If I could sum up most of my life in one phrase, it would be this: *constantly seeking approval.*

I've spent years striving to prove my worth—working hard to be the best, the most dependable, the most "together." When I look back at my past, I can see the thread running through so many of my stories—that quiet, relentless feeling of *less than*. And let me tell you, that will drive a Type A perfectionist absolutely crazy.

The words I've spoken to myself—both out loud and in my head—are things I wouldn't dream of saying to anyone else. That voice that says, *You're not doing enough. You're not good enough. You'll never be enough.* It's loud, cruel, and exhausting.

And before I go any further, let me say this: It wasn't because I wasn't loved. I was fiercely loved by my parents (and yes, I'm well aware I was the favorite child—we don't need to debate it). I had amazing friends. I knew Jesus. I had everything that should have made me feel secure.

But the enemy doesn't always attack what's visible—he goes for the unseen places. The quiet thoughts. The insecurities. The tender spots that still ache when no one's looking. He knew God's plans for my life were big (just like they are for *you*), and his only shot at sabotage was self-doubt.

He couldn't take away my calling—but if he could make me question it, he could keep me small.

Galatians 2:20 is the reminder that sets me free every time: *"I have been crucified with Christ, and I no longer live, but Christ lives in me."*

That means the striving, approval-chasing version of me doesn't have to run the show anymore. The one who constantly needed validation? She doesn't have the mic. Because the One who *loved me and gave Himself for me* already settled my worth once and for all.

I don't have to earn love that's already been given.

I don't have to perform for a God who already delights in me.

I don't have to chase approval that's already mine in Christ.

If you've been living in that same loop of "not enough," I get it. I've been there. But here's the truth I want you to hold onto—the voice of self-doubt may be loud, but it's not Lord.

Jesus is.

And His voice always speaks life, not lack.

Prayer:

Lord, thank You for loving me enough to silence the lies that say I'm not enough. Thank You that my worth is not found in what I achieve, but in who You are. Help me to live from Your love, not for approval, and remind me daily that I am already chosen, already loved, and already enough in You. Amen

DAY 18

Your Love Reaches the Heavens

> "Your love, Lord, reaches to the heavens, your faithfulness to the skies. Your righteousness is like the highest mountains, your justice like the great deep. You, Lord, preserve both people and animals. How priceless is your unfailing love, O God! People take refuge in the shadow of your wings." — *Psalm 36:5–7*

Have you ever had one of those moments where you just *stop*—maybe standing under a wide-open sky, looking at the ocean, or catching a sunset that feels like it was painted just for you—and think, *How does He love me this much?*

There's something about creation that reminds us just how big God really is. The sky stretches endlessly, the waves never stop coming, and the mountains stand strong through every season. And somehow, His love stretches even further than all of that.

That's hard for me to wrap my Type A, overthinking brain around. I like measurable things—numbers, goals, bullet points, plans. But this kind of love? It's immeasurable. It's not something I can schedule or track or earn. It just *is*. Constant. Boundless. Unfailing.

After years of chasing approval and trying to prove my worth, this verse hits differently. Because it tells me that God's love isn't limited by my performance, my past, or my pace. I can't out-succeed it, and I can't out-sin it. His love is as steady as the mountains and as infinite as the sky—and that's where my striving finally ends.

I've learned that the same God who created galaxies still notices when I'm overwhelmed on a Tuesday. The same God who holds the oceans in His hands also holds my anxious heart. His love doesn't shrink to fit my understanding—it expands to fill every space my fear tries to occupy.

That's why David called it *priceless*. Because there's nothing else like it—no love so steady, so forgiving, so unshakably faithful.

So, when life feels uncertain or your confidence starts to wobble, go outside. Look up. Let creation remind you of the Creator—and that His love for *you* reaches higher than anything you could ever imagine.

Prayer:
Lord, thank You for a love that is bigger than my fears, stronger than my failures, and wider than I can comprehend. Help me to see reminders of Your love all around me—in the sky, the mountains, and the simple moments of every day. Teach me to rest under the shadow of Your wings, knowing I am held by love that never ends. Amen.

DAY 19

Who Is a God Like You?

> "Who is a God like you, who pardons sin and forgives the transgression of the remnant of His inheritance? You do not stay angry forever but delight to show mercy." — *Micah 7:18*

I don't know about you, but sometimes I have a hard time forgiving *myself*.

I can talk about grace all day long—tell you how good God is, how His mercy never fails, how forgiveness is a gift. But when it comes to me? Well, that's a little harder to swallow.

I replay mistakes like old voicemail messages I should've deleted years ago. I overanalyze my words, my reactions, my should-haves and could-haves. And before I know it, I've turned guilt into a second job.

That's why this verse from Micah hits me right in the heart. *"Who is a God like you ... who delights to show mercy."*

Delights.

Not tolerates.

Not reluctantly agrees to forgive one more time.

He *delights* in it.

I think about how different that is from how we often respond. We extend forgiveness with a sigh, a warning, or a "don't do it again." But God forgives with joy—because restoring us brings Him joy.

I've messed up more times than I can count—said the wrong thing, acted out of fear, let pride get loud. But even in my worst moments, God doesn't roll His eyes and walk away. He steps closer. He calls me back.

And honestly, that kind of mercy blows my mind. Who does that? Who keeps forgiving when we keep fumbling? Who keeps loving when we keep doubting?

Only God.

When I think about my own story, I can see it everywhere—the times I thought I'd gone too far or failed too deeply, only to find His grace waiting for me at the end of my rope. Every single time, He's there, not with a lecture but with love.

If you've been carrying guilt or shame that's weighing you down, I want you to hear this: God isn't holding it over your head. He's holding out His hand.

You don't have to earn His forgiveness—you just have to accept it.

Because mercy isn't just something He gives. It's something He *is*.

Prayer:

Lord, thank You for being a God who delights in mercy. Thank You for forgiving me again and again, even when I struggle to forgive myself. Help me to stop replaying my regrets and start resting in Your grace. Teach me to extend that same mercy to others and to myself. Amen.

DAY 20

This Is Love

> "This is love: not that we loved God, but that He loved us and sent His Son as an atoning sacrifice for our sins." — *1 John 4:10*

If you've ever tried to earn someone's love—or hold onto it by being "enough"—you know how exhausting that can be.

We live in a world where love often comes with fine print. *I'll love you if you behave, if you agree, if you don't disappoint me, if you earn it.* And for a long time, I treated God's love the same way.

If I prayed enough.
If I served enough.
If I performed well enough.
If I was perfect enough.
Then maybe I'd finally be lovable enough.

But that's not what 1 John 4:10 says. This verse doesn't describe a love we achieved—it defines a love that found us first. *"Not that we loved God, but that He loved us."*

That means before you ever said His name, He said yours. Before you took your first step toward Him, He was already walking toward you. Before you ever tried to prove your worth, He had already declared it.

It's hard to wrap my head around sometimes. Because I'm a "doer." I like a checklist. I want to contribute. But God's love is the one thing I can't add to or improve upon. It's complete all by itself—no performance required.

I think back to all the times I've felt unworthy—the times I've tried to clean myself up before coming to Him, the times I've whispered, *"You probably love everyone else more than me."* And yet, every time, His response is the same:

"Amy, this is love—not that you loved Me, but that I loved you."

That's it. No loopholes. No earning. No proving. Just love—steady, sacrificial, and scandalously unconditional.

So, if you've been running yourself ragged trying to be lovable, stop. You already are. Not because of what you've done, but because of who He is.

That's what real love looks like.

That's what this is—love.

Prayer:

Lord, thank You for loving me first. Thank You that Your love doesn't depend on my performance, my progress, or my perfection. Help me to rest in the truth that I am already loved—completely and without condition. Let that truth shape the way I love others today. Amen.

DAY 21

Loved First

"We love because He first loved us." — 1 John 4:19

There's so much freedom packed into this tiny verse. Six simple words that flip the entire idea of love upside down: *We love because He first loved us.*

Not "we love so He'll love us."

Not "we love to prove we're worthy."

Not "we love because it's our job."

No—we love because *He loved first.*

When I think about this verse, I always come back to something my mom used to say to me growing up: *"I love God most so I can love you better."*

It didn't make much sense to me when I was younger. I mean, how could loving someone else *more* help you love *me* better? But now I get it. What she was really saying was that when our love starts with God, it flows differently. It's deeper. Stronger. "Better."

When we start from being loved by Him, everything else we give comes from overflow—not exhaustion.

I've lived plenty of seasons where I tried to pour from an empty cup, where I loved people from a place of striving instead of security. I gave to be seen, served to feel needed, and loved to be loved back. And you know what? It never worked. Because love that doesn't start with God eventually runs out.

But love that starts with Him? It's endless.

When you know you're already loved—not because of what you do, but because of who you belong to—you don't have to chase affection or approval. You can love freely, without keeping score. You can forgive without resentment. You can show up for people even when they can't show up for you.

Because you're not loving *for* something.

You're loving *from* something—from Him.

And that changes everything.

So today, before you rush into your to-do list or try to meet everyone else's needs, pause for a second and let this truth sink in: You are already loved. You have nothing to earn and nothing to prove. Let His love fill you first—and then go love the world from that place.

Prayer:
Lord, thank You for loving me first—before I even knew how to love You back. Help me to live from that love, not for it. Fill me so full of Your presence that it naturally overflows into how I treat others. Teach me to love from abundance, not emptiness. Amen.

DAY 22

Abounding in Love

"But You, Lord, are a compassionate and gracious God, slow to anger, abounding in love and faithfulness." — Psalm 86:15

There's something about that word—*abounding*.

It doesn't mean *enough*. It means *overflowing*. More than you could ever use up.

I love that this verse doesn't just say God has love; it says He's *abounding* in it. The picture that comes to mind is a cup that just keeps spilling over, no matter how many times you try to drink it dry.

That's comforting for a woman like me—a recovering perfectionist who still has her moments of impatience, overreaction, or second-guessing. Because my love, on my best days, has limits. It gets tired. It runs out. His doesn't.

If you've ever loved someone who made it hard, or tried to show grace when your emotions wanted to do anything *but* grace, you know how quickly human love can fray. But God's love? It doesn't fray. It doesn't fade. It doesn't hinge on your performance or your progress.

He's slow to anger—even when we rush headfirst into the same mistakes.

He's gracious—even when we forget to be grateful.

And He's abounding in love—even when ours runs short.

When I think back over my life, I can trace His patience in

every chapter. In the waiting seasons. In the wandering ones. In the "What on earth am I doing?" years. His love didn't just stick around—it expanded. It grew to meet every new version of me that needed it.

Maybe that's what abounding love really is: love that adapts without diminishing, that stretches without snapping, that holds steady no matter how much weight you put on it.

So if you're in a season where you feel like you've used up all your grace—with yourself or with others—remember this: God's supply hasn't changed. He's still patient. Still kind. Still abounding. And His overflow is more than enough to refill yours.

Prayer:

Lord, thank You for being patient when I'm impatient, gracious when I'm stubborn, and abounding in love when mine runs thin. Teach me to receive from Your overflow so I can love others with the same gentleness and grace You've shown me. Amen.

DAY 23

Love Covers

> "Above all, love each other deeply, because love covers over a multitude of sins." — *1 Peter 4:8*

My mom used to say to me, "I love you anyways."

Now, let me be clear—I was a pretty good kid. (Some might even say the self-proclaimed *favorite* child, but we won't open that debate again.) Still, even the "favorite" has her moments. I could throw a tantrum with Olympic precision, talk back with confidence I hadn't earned, say I had completed something I planned on doing later and let's just say there were seasons where my halo needed polishing.

But no matter how many times I tested her patience, my mom's response was the same: "I love you anyways."

Those four words shaped me more than I realized. They meant her love wasn't dependent on my behavior, my attitude, or how "together" I was that day. Her love wasn't blind to my flaws—it just refused to be defined by them.

And that's what Peter was talking about in this verse. *"Love each other deeply, because love covers over a multitude of sins."*

Now, covering doesn't mean pretending the wrong never happened or sweeping it under the rug. It means choosing compassion over condemnation. It means seeing the full picture of someone—the good, the bad, and the "oh, Lord, help them"—and deciding to love them anyways.

God's love covers us that way every single day. Not because we've earned it, but because that's who He is. And when we live from that kind of love, we start extending it to others—even when they make it hard.

There's something powerful about loving someone "anyways." It doesn't excuse behavior, but it mirrors grace. It says, "You're not perfect, but neither am I—and I'm choosing love over keeping score."

That kind of love changes relationships. It softens hearts. It builds bridges. And sometimes, it's the only sermon someone will ever hear.

So today, whether it's your family, your coworkers, or that one person who seems to have a spiritual gift for testing your patience, remember: Love them anyways. Because that's what love does—it covers.

Prayer:

Lord, thank You for loving me anyways—through my attitude, mistakes, and imperfections. Teach me to love others with that same grace. When I'm tempted to judge or hold a grudge, remind me that love doesn't ignore the mess—it moves toward it. Help me reflect the covering kind of love You've shown me. Amen.

DAY 24

Never Out of His Reach

> "Where can I go from your Spirit?
> Where can I flee from your presence?
> If I go up to the heavens, you are there;
> if I make my bed in the depths, you are there.
> If I rise on the wings of the dawn,
> if I settle on the far side of the sea,
> even there your hand will guide me,
> your right hand will hold me fast."
> — *Psalm 139:7–10*

There are some verses in Scripture that feel like a warm hand on your shoulder—the kind that steadies you, calms you, and reminds you that you're not as alone as you feel. Psalm 139 does that for me every single time.

I love how David doesn't ask this like a question—he already knows the answer.

There is nowhere you can go where God is not already there.

He lists it out just so we don't miss it:

Heaven? He's there.

Rock bottom? Still there.

A brand new sunrise? There.

The far side of the sea where you've convinced yourself you've escaped everything familiar?

Yeah ... He's there too.

And not just present—guiding. Holding. Keeping.

I've had seasons where that truth felt comforting, and seasons where it felt ... honestly, inconvenient. Times when I wandered, doubted, avoided, hid—moments where I thought maybe I'd finally found the one corner of life where God would say, "All right, girl ... that's enough. You're on your own."

But that's not who He is.

He doesn't wait for you to come back home to love you.

He loves you *while you're running.*

He holds you *while you're falling.*

He guides you *while you're trying to pretend you don't need guidance.*

His presence doesn't break when you break.

It doesn't vanish when you're overwhelmed.

It doesn't evaporate when your choices get messy or your faith gets thin.

David isn't just offering reassurance—he's making a declaration:

"I've been high, I've been low, I've been lost, I've been wrong ... and in every single place, He was there."

Maybe you're in a season right now where you feel far from God—not because He moved, but because life did. Maybe shame told you to hide. Maybe exhaustion convinced you to retreat. Maybe fear whispered that you'd wandered too far.

But hear this:

You are never beyond His reach.

You couldn't outrun His presence if you tried.

Even there—wherever your "there" is—His hand is guiding you, and His right hand is holding you fast.

Take a breath, friend.

You are held.

You are seen.

You are never, ever alone.

Prayer

Lord, thank You that there is nowhere I can go where Your presence doesn't meet me. When I wander, when I worry, when I hide, remind me that You are still holding me fast. Help me rest in the truth that I am never out of Your reach and never outside of Your love. Amen.

DAY 25

Perfect Love Casts Out Fear

> "There is no fear in love. But perfect love drives out fear, because fear has to do with punishment. The one who fears is not made perfect in love." — *1 John 4:18*

In my book *Just Brave It*, I call myself a "brave expert."

But here's the thing about being an expert—you only get there by *practice*. And in order to practice bravery, you first have to feel fear. You can't be brave without it. Fear is the entry fee for courage.

For years, I thought bravery meant being fearless—like the women who charge into big moments without hesitation, smiling in the face of uncertainty. Turns out, that's not bravery. That's denial. Real bravery is when your knees are shaking, your heart's pounding, and you do the thing anyway.

And I'll be honest—I spent a lot of time *not* doing the thing.

When I wasn't walking in God's purpose for my life, I spent more time feeling fear than freedom. I let doubt lead the conversation. I let "what if" win the argument. And I got pretty comfortable sitting in the safe zone—until God, in His love and perfect timing, smacked me over the head a time or two to get my attention. (He's gentle, but He's also persistent. Sometimes He's got to knock a girl out of her comfort zone.)

What I've learned is that God's love doesn't just comfort you in fear—it *casts it out*.

Because fear thrives in the absence of love. When you're unsure of who you are, or uncertain of who He is, fear has room to grow. But the moment His perfect love fills the space, fear loses its footing.

The closer you get to His love, the smaller fear becomes.

Perfect love doesn't mean everything feels perfect. It means you're anchored in something stronger than your circumstances. It means you don't have to have all the answers to take the next step. It means you can be scared and brave at the same time—because you know the One leading you is trustworthy.

So if fear's been loud lately—about your calling, your future, or your next step—remember this: Fear might knock, but love always answers louder.

You don't have to wait until you feel fearless to move forward. Just let His love lead you there—one brave step at a time.

Prayer:
Lord, thank You that Your love doesn't just comfort me—it drives out fear. When I start to shrink back or let "what if" win, remind me that courage isn't the absence of fear; it's trusting You in the middle of it. Help me to walk boldly in Your purpose for my life, grounded in Your perfect love. Amen.

DAY 26

Above All

> "And above all these put on love, which binds everything together in perfect harmony." — *Colossians 3:14*

If you know me, you know I *love* clothes. Like, really, really love them.

I'm that girl who plans outfits in advance, who knows the exact shoes that go with the exact earrings, and who firmly believes a good blazer can solve 90% of life's problems. Everything I put on is well thought out—sometimes dreamed about long before I actually wear it.

So when Paul says, *"Above all, put on love,"* I can't help but think of it like getting dressed—intentional, daily, and necessary.

He's not talking about an optional accessory here. Love isn't the last bracelet you add at the end to elevate the outfit. It's the whole outfit. The thing that ties it all together.

Because without love, everything else starts to fall apart.

Patience without love becomes quiet resentment.

Kindness without love turns into obligation.

Truth without love feels like judgment.

But when you "put on" love first—when it's the layer closest to your heart—everything else you wear in life fits better. Your words soften. Your priorities shift. Your interactions carry grace instead of edge.

And here's the key: *Putting on love* takes intention. You don't wake up wearing it. Just like getting dressed, it's a choice—every day. There are mornings when "putting on love" feels as easy as slipping into your favorite sweater. And there are others when it feels like trying to zip up jeans that no longer want to cooperate.

But those are the days we need love the most—not just to cover us, but to hold us together.

Because love really is the glue. It's what keeps families from falling apart, friendships from breaking down, and our faith from becoming hollow. Above all the things we could wear—grace, forgiveness, compassion—love is what binds them in harmony.

So tomorrow morning, when you're standing in front of your closet deciding what to wear, take a second to remember what matters most. Before you pick the shoes or the accessories, start with this: *Put on love.*

It always looks good on you and never goes out of style.

Prayer:

Lord, thank You for reminding me that love is the one thing that holds everything together. Help me to "put on" love first—in my thoughts, my words, and my actions. Teach me to lead with love in every decision and interaction, and let it be the thing that defines me more than anything I wear. Amen.

DAY 27

New Every Morning

> "Because of the Lord's great love we are not consumed, for His compassions never fail. They are new every morning; great is Your faithfulness." — *Lamentations 3:22–23*

There are few things I love more than a fresh start—a clean slate, a quiet morning, and that first sip of coffee that somehow makes the whole world feel right again.

If you're like me, you go to bed excited about your coffee in the morning and a deep appreciation for a good second cup. And honestly? That's kind of how I picture God's mercy. A constant, never-ending pour that fills you back up right when you think you've run dry.

This verse from *Lamentations* says His mercies are *new every morning*. Not recycled. Not reheated leftovers from yesterday. *New.*

Think about that. Every single day, you wake up to a fresh delivery of grace. You don't have to ration it, earn it, or try to make yesterday's supply stretch. His compassion doesn't come with a limit or an expiration date.

And if we're being real—some days, I need more refills than others. There are days I feel like a fully charged iPhone at 8:00 a.m., and by lunchtime, I'm running on 2% with three missed calls, forty-two unread texts, and no charger in sight.

But that's the beauty of God's love—it's the ultimate recharge. His mercy meets you where you are, no matter how drained, distracted, or disappointed you feel. It whispers, *"Yesterday's gone. Today's new. Let's begin again."*

Because of His love, we are *not consumed*. Not by our mistakes. Not by our worries. Not by the weight we carry. His faithfulness doesn't flicker with our feelings; it's steady.

So whatever yesterday held—the regret, the overwhelm, the mess you swore you'd clean up but didn't—let it go. You've got new grace today. And guess what? You'll get more tomorrow.

You can't use it up. You can only wake up to it.

Prayer:
Lord, thank You for fresh mercy that meets me every morning. Thank You that I never wake up empty-handed—Your love restocks my heart daily. Help me to let go of yesterday and step into today with peace, gratitude, and grace for myself and others. Amen.

DAY 28

Love That Covers

> "Hatred stirs up conflict, but love covers all wrongs." — *Proverbs 10:12*

We live in a world that loves a good argument. Scroll for two minutes online, and you'll find people fighting about everything—opinions, politics, parking spots, you name it. It's exhausting.

But Proverbs 10:12 reminds us of something simple and radical: *"Hatred stirs up conflict, but love covers all wrongs."*

Love doesn't ignore pain—it mends it. It doesn't sweep things under the rug—it invites healing. It doesn't mean pretending the hurt never happened. It means choosing grace instead of getting even.

Let's be honest—when someone wrongs you, the first instinct isn't usually, "You know what I'm going to do? Love them!" Nope. It's to protect yourself. Maybe clap back a little. Maybe hold on to that silent resentment. But love that *covers* isn't about weakness—it's about strength. It takes more courage to choose compassion than it does to carry bitterness.

And covering doesn't mean excusing the wrong. It means refusing to let the wrong define the relationship—or your heart.

When we choose love, we stop the cycle of hurt. We trade payback for peace. We mirror the same grace that's been poured over us time and time again.

Because truthfully, God could've kept score with us—but He didn't. Instead, He covered us with mercy.

So, the next time someone makes it hard to love them (and let's be honest, that person might show up before lunch), take a deep breath. Choose love over being right. Choose peace over proving your point. Choose to cover, not to compete.

Love doesn't just calm the conflict—it heals the wound.

Prayer:

Lord, thank You for loving me enough to cover my wrongs. Teach me to extend that same grace to others. When my pride wants to react, help me to respond in love instead. Make my heart quick to forgive, slow to take offense, and ready to heal instead of hurt. Amen.

DAY 29

Love That Pursues

> "But while he was still a long way off, his father saw him and was filled with compassion for him; he ran to his son, threw his arms around him and kissed him." — *Luke 15:20*

There are few verses in the Bible that show the heart of God more clearly than this one.

The story of the Prodigal Son isn't just about a son who wandered—it's about a Father who *ran*.

I love that detail. The father didn't sit on the porch, arms crossed, waiting for his son to grovel. He didn't say, "Well, let's see how sorry he really is." He saw his boy *while he was still a long way off*—meaning the son hadn't even made it home yet—and the father *ran* to him.

That's what God's love looks like. It pursues. It runs toward us when we're still messy, still unsure, still halfway between "I want to come home" and "I don't deserve to."

I've been there—standing in that in-between space, wondering if I've gone too far or failed too many times. But every time, God has met me the same way: not with a lecture, but with open arms.

That's the beauty of His love. It doesn't wait for perfection; it runs toward repentance. It's not cautious or conditional—it's wholehearted and wild.

Sometimes, I think we expect God to love us the way people

do—a little hesitant, a little measured, maybe waiting to see if we'll prove ourselves. But His love doesn't calculate. It moves first.

If you've been feeling distant from God, hear this: He hasn't gone anywhere. In fact, He's already running your way.

You don't have to earn your way back. You just have to take one step—and you'll find He's already halfway toward meet you.

Because that's who He is—a God who pursues. A Father who runs. A love that never stops chasing after you.

Prayer:

Lord, thank You for being a God who runs toward me, not away from me. Thank You that Your love meets me in the middle of my mess and welcomes me home every time. Help me to rest in the truth that I am always pursued, always wanted, and always loved by You. Amen.

DAY 30

Love That Holds

> "So do not fear, for I am with you; do not be dismayed, for I am your God. I will strengthen you and help you; I will uphold you with my righteous right hand." — *Isaiah 41:10*

Some loves comfort you. Some cheer for you.

But the love of God? It *holds* you.

And not just when life is going smoothly—but especially when it's not.

I love how this verse in Isaiah isn't a suggestion—it's a promise. *"Do not fear ... I will uphold you."* It doesn't say, "I might help if I have time," or "Once you've pulled yourself together, I'll step in." Nope. It's clear, steady, and absolute: *I've got you.*

If you've ever had a season where you felt like you were holding on by a thread—where the to-do list was longer than your patience, or the weight of life felt like too much—you know how powerful that truth is.

God doesn't just *help* you hold it together; He *is* what holds you together.

His love is the unseen grip that steadies you when you start to unravel. The gentle whisper that says, *"You're not doing this alone."* The strength that shows up right when yours runs out.

It reminds me of when I was teaching my sons to walk as babies. They stumbled, wobbled, and nearly fell over and over, but every time, my hand was right there. Steady. Sure. Protective. That's God's love—not removing the stumbles, but holding you through them.

Maybe today you're facing something that feels uncertain or heavy. Maybe you've prayed for clarity and gotten silence. Or maybe you're just plain tired. Whatever it is, hear this—you're not falling apart. You're being held.

You don't have to have a perfect grip on God; His grip on you is enough.

So breathe. Unclench your fists. Stop striving to hold it all up by yourself. Let His love do the holding.

Because His hands, the ones that shaped the universe, are the same hands holding you.

Prayer:

Lord, thank You for being the steady hand that holds me when life feels unstable. When fear creeps in or my strength gives out, remind me that Your love never lets go. Help me rest in the safety of Your grip and find peace knowing I am secure in You. Amen.

HIS PLAN

His Plan

You've spent the last thirty days soaking in the truth of *His Love*—not the kind we quote on a coffee mug, but the kind that meets you in the mess, sits with you in the waiting room, and still calls you *worthy* when you feel anything but.

You've begun to see that your value was never something you had to earn. It's not tied to your performance, your past, or how "together" your life looks. It's rooted in the simple, stunning truth that the Creator of the universe chose you—and still does, every single day.

Now that you know how deeply you're loved, it's time to ask: *"If that's true… then what does He have planned for me?"*

Because once you understand your worth in His love, you begin to see that *His plan* isn't punishment—it's purpose. It's the unfolding of a story written by someone who knows your heart better than you do.

And no, it's not always neat or predictable. Sometimes His plan looks like closed doors, detours, or waiting seasons that make zero sense. But it's in those very moments that your faith and your worth start to intertwine—where you stop striving to prove yourself and start trusting that you were *made* for something intentional.

So as we step into this next section, *His Plan*, take a deep breath and remember:

You are already loved.

You are already chosen.

And because of that, you can walk forward knowing that whatever comes next has already been written with love.

His love defined your *value*.

Now His plan will reveal your *purpose*.

DAY 31

Plans That Prosper

> "For I know the plans I have for you," declares the Lord, "plans to prosper you and not to harm you, plans to give you hope and a future." — *Jeremiah 29:11*

This verse first took hold of my heart when I was asked to speak at the inaugural prayer breakfast during the International Builders' Show. My topic that morning was simple but honest—*what women in our industry most needed prayer for.*

And what came up over and over again was advancement.

Promotion.

Purpose.

The desire to move forward—in our careers, in our confidence, in our calling.

But as I prayed and prepared, God kept pressing this verse on my heart. And when I stood on that stage, I shared what I now know was *for me* just as much as it was for them:

That prayer for advancement? It's already been answered.

Because God has already promised it—just not always in the way we picture it.

His "plans to prosper you" aren't about job titles, salary bands, or LinkedIn announcements. They're about peace. The kind of prosperity that happens inside your soul when you know you're walking in step with Him, even when the outside world doesn't see the promotion yet.

I didn't know it then, but that message was preparing me for a long season of whispers—seasons where God was giving me incredible opportunities but still quietly saying, "This isn't your room."

I'd stand on stages, lead teams, record podcasts, even deliver a TEDx talk—and hear that same voice. *"I'm giving you this opportunity to prepare you, but this is not what I have for you."*

It didn't make sense. It was hard to keep showing up when I didn't understand what He was doing. But looking back now, I can see it so clearly—He wasn't holding me back; He was building me up.

Because sometimes the plan that feels stalled is really the plan that's being shaped.

Sometimes what feels like *not yet* is actually *you're not ready.*

And sometimes, the only way to prosper is to pause—long enough for Him to realign your purpose with His.

If you're in that space right now—showing up, doing the work, but still hearing, *"This isn't your room"* —hold on. You're not missing it. You're in preparation for it.

God's plans for your life are still active, still advancing, still good.

Even when you can't see them prospering on paper—they're prospering your heart.

Prayer:

Lord, thank You for the plans You've written over my life—even when I can't yet see how they'll unfold. When I start to measure progress by titles, numbers, or timelines, remind me that Your prosperity is about peace. Teach me to trust Your timing, even in the quiet, and to keep showing up faithfully in every room You send me to—even the ones that are just preparation. Amen.

DAY 32

Called for More

> "For we are God's handiwork, created in Christ Jesus to do good works, which God prepared in advance for us to do." — *Ephesians 2:10*

There's a quiet ache that comes when you feel like everyone else is moving forward—when you're watching others step into their calling while you're stuck wondering if you somehow missed yours.

I know that feeling all too well.

For months, I lived in that strange in-between—the space between *knowing* God was calling me to something more, and *not knowing* what that actually looked like. And honestly, being afraid that I wasn't worthy and even if I was that I didn't want it.

This both frustrated me and, in fact, scared me. Because I wanted clarity. I wanted direction. And ministry, at least how I pictured it, didn't feel like my lane. I didn't see how what I was doing through *Just Brave It* could possibly fit into that world. I loved Jesus deeply, but I was afraid that "ministry" might push people away from Him instead of drawing them in.

So I did what most of us do when we don't know what to do—I froze. I stopped creating. I stopped building. I felt stuck, paralyzed between what was and what could be.

Then, a few weeks ago, I attended an event for women in my industry, the kind of event I usually speak at. I sat in a room of 250 women listening to another speaker who, interestingly enough, was also a TEDx speaker and author AND working to empower women in my industry. As I listened, that same overwhelming sense returned—*this is not your room.*

And this time, it hit differently.

The next morning, I woke up early and just lay there, replaying the same thought over and over again: *I feel like I'm behind.*

I didn't say it out loud—but I didn't have to. God heard it.

Eventually, I got up and went downstairs, planning to have quiet time, but instead, I started typing. I poured everything I was feeling—the fear, the confusion, the calling, the paralysis—into ChatGPT. (And before you say it, yes, I know. God doesn't need AI to get His point across, but He sure isn't afraid to use it either.)

As I read back what it generated, there was one line that stopped me cold:

"You are not behind; you are being set apart."

It wasn't something I'd written. I hadn't even hinted at it. But it was the exact phrase that had been looping in my mind just thirty minutes earlier as I lay in bed, thinking, *I feel like I'm getting left behind.*

And in that moment, I felt it—the still, undeniable voice of God saying, *"Daughter, I heard you. You're not behind. You're being prepared."*

That moment reminded me of something I've learned again and again—calling isn't about spotlight; it's about obedience.

It's not about how fast you move, how visible you are, or how far along you think you should be. It's about trusting that the One who made you—the same God who handcrafted your personality, your story, your gifts, and even your quirks—already prepared the work you're meant to do.

You are not random.

You are not late.

You are not forgotten.

You are called for more.

So if you've been feeling stuck, unseen, or behind—take heart. You're not missing your moment; God is shaping it. And when the time is right, it won't pass you by.

Prayer:

Lord, thank You for reminding me that I was created on purpose for a purpose. When I start to compare my journey to others or feel like I'm falling behind, remind me that You're not done with me—You're developing me. Help me to trust the process, listen for Your voice, and say yes to the "more" You're calling me into, one step at a time. Amen.

DAY 33

Divine Detours (My Burning Bush Moment)

> "In their hearts humans plan their course, but the Lord establishes their steps." — *Proverbs 16:9*

If you've ever made a five-year plan and then watched God laugh, you'll feel right at home here.

I'm a planner by nature. I like goals, strategy, calendar—a color-coded road map for my life. But God? He apparently prefers scenic routes.

After weeks of feeling His whisper—that *"not your room"* voice—and then the gentle nudge through that *"you are not behind; you are being set apart"* moment, I thought maybe, finally, I was starting to understand the direction.

Then came the detour.

I was sitting at my desk one afternoon when an email popped up for a major industry event—the kind of event I used to be part of, led by people I admire and call friends. When the idea for it first came up, a few of them had even said, *"Amy, we want you involved. You're the heart of this."*

But here I was, reading the announcement, and my name was nowhere on it.

Even though I knew deep down it wasn't *my* room—God had already made that clear—it still stung. The questions started rolling in fast and ugly: *Did they not think I was good enough? Did I do something wrong? Am I being left behind?*

You know that slump-over-your-desk posture of defeat? That was me.

And right in that moment, when the self-doubt was loudest, God rerouted me again—this time with a full-on, unmistakable, divine smack to the head.

Out of nowhere, I remembered a notification I'd seen earlier that morning. I picked up my phone, opened my *Just Brave It* email, and saw two unread messages. One was from a friend. The other—from Jamie Kern Lima, author of *Worthy*.

Now listen, Jamie's book came out around the same time as mine. Except she knows Oprah and has a huge following. I, on the other hand, was just over here "braving it." I'd joined her email list mostly for research and, being human, had about 150 unread messages from her sitting in my inbox. But for some reason (God), I felt prompted to click this one.

The subject line read: **"The Most Life-Changing Advice I've Ever Heard."**

And inside were the words that made my jaw hit the desk:

"**You are not behind; you're being prepared**.

What felt like a delay was divine preparation.

What felt like rejection was redirection.

What felt like the end was the beginning of something more beautiful than you could have imagined."

I just sat there whispering, *"Okay, God ... I see You."*

"You are not behind" —the words I spoke to myself, the words he used to confirm my next steps, and now the **exact** ones he would use to finally give me my burning bush I had so desperately been praying for.

In that moment, I realized what I thought was rejection was

actually protection—a detour designed to keep me from settling for less than His best.

Because here's the thing about divine detours: They don't always come with warning signs. They often show up as closed doors, delayed opportunities, or unanswered emails. But every single one still leads you exactly where He wants you to go.

When I finally looked up from that email, I could almost hear God chuckling—*"How many times do I have to tell you, Amy?"*

His plans aren't random. They're rerouted on purpose. And when He says *no* to something good, it's only because He's saying *yes* to something better.

So the next time your plan gets derailed, remember—you're not off course. You're on God's detour, and He's still the one holding the map.

Prayer:

Lord, thank You for every detour that saved me from less than Your best. When my plans fall apart or my confidence wavers, remind me that You are never late and never lost. Help me trade control for surrender and trust that every redirection is really preparation for something better. Amen.

DAY 34

The Waiting Room

> "Wait for the Lord; be strong and take heart and wait for the Lord." — *Psalm 27:14*

There's a special kind of uncomfortable that comes with waiting.

It's like sitting in the world's longest line—you can't speed it up, you can't skip ahead, and for the love of all that's holy, you can't figure out why the person at the front is taking so long.

Waiting on God feels a lot like that sometimes, doesn't it?

You know He's good. You know He's faithful. But when the prayers seem unanswered and the progress feels slow, it's easy to start wondering if maybe He forgot to call your name.

And you know by now I've been there—more than once. And if we're being real, I don't wait gracefully. I fidget. I plan. I over-analyze. I ask, *"How long?"* about twelve different ways. I want answers, movement, and clarity. But here's what I've learned the hard way: Waiting is never wasted when God's the One who's making you wait.

The waiting room is where He strengthens your heart before He stretches your calling. It's where He matures what your emotions can't yet carry. It's where He develops the discipline, humility, and faith you'll need for what's next.

You might not see the progress yet—but something is *always* happening in the unseen.

Maybe you're in that space right now—where things look quiet on the surface, but deep down, your heart is restless. You're watching others step into their purpose while you feel like you're still in the lobby, holding your number, waiting for your turn.

Can I remind you of something?

You're not forgotten. You're being *formed*.

That's what Psalm 27:14 is all about. "Wait for the Lord" isn't a suggestion; it's an invitation—not to sit idly, but to stay *ready*.

Waiting on God doesn't mean doing nothing. It means refusing to move until He moves. It means choosing trust over timelines and peace over panic.

Because when the waiting ends, and it will, you'll realize what felt like delay was actually preparation. Every silent day was strengthening your faith for what's ahead.

So, take heart. Be strong. And if all you can do today is sit still and whisper, *"I'm still here, Lord,"* that's enough. He's not late. He's just building the kind of foundation that doesn't crack under pressure.

Prayer:

Lord, thank You for meeting me in the waiting room. When I grow restless or impatient, remind me that this season isn't punishment—it's preparation. Help me to find peace in the pause and strength in the stillness, trusting that Your timing is perfect and Your plan is worth the wait. Amen.

DAY 35

The God Who Orders Steps

> "The Lord makes firm the steps of the one who delights in Him." — *Psalm 37:23*

If you're anything like me, you like a good plan. Preferably color-coded, time-stamped, and in bullet points.

But God? He's more of a *"trust Me for the next turn"* kind of planner.

When God gave me my burning bush moment—that clear, can't-deny-it confirmation of the calling He'd been whispering to my heart—I was ready. Fired up. Purpose downloaded. Passion fully ignited.

I leaned in, and my heart was on fire.

And then ... reality.

Because what I *expected* was a straight path. What I *got* was a series of steps. Tiny, faithful, day-by-day steps that didn't always make sense. I knew the path but the work to get there couldn't be done overnight.

I wanted the map; He handed me a compass.

I wanted the full itinerary; He said, *"Let's start with one step."*

And maybe that's where you are, too. You've had glimpses of purpose. You've felt those holy nudges. Maybe you've even had your own "burning bush" moment—something that lit your soul up and reminded you that God has something more for you.

But now, you're standing in the afterglow thinking, *"Okay ... now what?"*

Here's what I'm learning—God rarely gives us the whole plan because we'd either sprint ahead or talk ourselves out of it. He gives us *the next step,* because He wants our trust more than our strategy.

Psalm 37:23 says, "The Lord makes firm the steps of the one who delights in Him."

Notice it doesn't say the *leaps.*

He doesn't ask for perfect pacing, just a heart that's willing to keep walking with Him.

The truth is, even after that big "aha" moment in my life, I still have days where I question, hesitate, or second-guess. I'm still learning to trust—and if you are too, that's okay.

God isn't grading your faith on distance covered; He's looking at your direction.

He knows your heart.

He knows the plan.

And He's not going to let you miss it.

So even if your steps feel small, wobbly, or unsure—take them anyway. Because when you delight in Him, every single one lands on solid ground.

You don't need to see the whole map to move forward. You just need to trust the One holding it.

Prayer:

Lord, thank You for ordering my steps, even when I can't see the full path. When I get impatient or afraid, remind me that my job is obedience—not control. Help me to delight in You more than my destination and to walk in faith, one small, steady step at a time. Amen.

DAY 36

From Chaos to Clarity

> "And we know that in all things God works for the good of those who love Him, who have been called according to His purpose." — *Romans 8:28*

Here's something I've learned the hard way: Clarity doesn't come before obedience—it comes through it.

And sometimes, right before we step into the very thing God has been preparing us for, life feels like it's falling apart.

That's not coincidence—it's often confirmation.

Because when you start walking closer to your purpose, the enemy gets nervous. Spiritual warfare doesn't usually show up with flashing lights or full-on exorcist moments—it's often subtle.

It's distraction.

It's discouragement.

It's that whisper of *"You're not ready,"* or *"You're not enough."*

It's the exhaustion that hits right when you've found momentum.

If you've been feeling that lately, like every step forward gets met with pushback, take heart. It's not a sign that you're off track. It's proof that you're walking toward something holy.

There will be missteps and step-backs along the way. There will be days when obedience feels like chaos and faith feels like a free fall. You'll question the timing, the purpose, maybe even the calling itself.

But here's the thing about God—He wastes nothing.

Even the detours, even the heartbreaks, even the days you feel too weary to keep going—all of it gets folded into His plan. Romans 8:28 doesn't say *some* things work together for good. It says *all* things.

That means the doors that closed.

The seasons that broke you.

The mistakes you still cringe over.

The moments that made no sense at all.

They're all part of the story He's writing through you.

So, if today feels heavy or confusing, if the plan feels hidden and your faith feels small, keep showing up anyway. You don't have to see how it all fits. You just have to trust that it does.

Because the same God who spoke purpose over your life before you ever took your first breath is still working behind the scenes.

He is coming.

He is moving.

And when the time is right, He will reveal His plan with the kind of clarity that only comes after chaos.

Hold tight. He's not done yet.

Prayer:

Lord, thank You for being the God who brings order out of chaos and meaning out of mess. When life feels uncertain or the enemy tries to distract me with doubt, remind me that You're still in control. Help me to stay steadfast in the waiting, to trust You in the battle, and to believe that every setback is still leading me closer to Your plan. Amen.

DAY 37

Kingdom Timing

> "There is a time for everything, and a season for every activity under the heavens." — *Ecclesiastes 3:1*

I'll be honest ... patience isn't exactly my spiritual superpower.

If God had a "track my order" feature for prayers, I'd use it daily.

Because I like things to move.

I like progress, clarity, checklists. I want to see the plan unfolding in real time. But God doesn't work on *Amazon Prime* timelines—He works on Kingdom time. And Kingdom time rarely matches our calendar.

After my burning bush moment, after the detours, and after the waiting, I thought, *Okay, Lord, I'm ready. Let's do this thing.*

And then ... silence.

Stillness.

The kind of holy pause that makes you start wondering if maybe you misheard Him.

But here's what I've learned (and continue to relearn): Just because it's not happening *yet* doesn't mean it's not happening.

Ecclesiastes 3:1 reminds us that there is a *time for everything*. Not just the visible, exciting parts, but the hidden, developing ones too. The slow seasons. The quiet ones. The ones where it feels like everyone else is sprinting ahead while you're standing still, asking, *"Did I miss my moment?"*

You didn't miss it.

You're right on schedule.

God's timeline isn't delayed, it's divine. He knows exactly what needs to grow in you before He can grow something through you.

And if you're anything like me, that truth requires daily surrender. Because my flesh wants the highlight reel, but God cares more about the heart work. He's not just arranging circumstances; He's shaping character.

Sometimes His "not yet" is protecting you from a version of success you're not ready to carry.

Sometimes His pause is positioning someone else who needs to be part of your story.

And sometimes, He's just letting you rest before the next stretch of brave.

Whatever season you're in—slow, silent, stretching, or steady—it's not wasted. It's working. And one day, when you look back, you'll see how every delay was divine design.

So take a breath.

You're not behind.

You're being prepared, right on time.

Prayer:

Lord, thank You that Your timing is perfect, even when it feels painfully slow. Help me to trust the pace You've set for my life and to find beauty in this season, not just the next one. Remind me that I'm not behind—I'm right where You want me, walking in Kingdom time. Amen.

DAY 38

Surrendered Plans

> "Father, if You are willing, take this cup from Me; yet not My will, but Yours be done." — *Luke 22:42*

Let's just say this up front—surrender sounds beautiful in worship lyrics, but it feels a whole lot harder in real life.

Because letting go means losing control, and for people like me (and maybe you too), control feels safe. Predictable. Manageable. Until it's not.

God has this way of lovingly unraveling the plans we make for ourselves—not to punish us, but to protect us from smaller stories than the one He's writing.

I've had moments where I've looked around and thought, *"This is not what I planned."*

The job that didn't work out.

The relationship that ended.

The dream that shifted.

The path that looked nothing like the one I mapped out.

And yet ... when I look closer, I can see how God's fingerprints were all over the redirections. The heartbreaks that humbled me. The detours that developed me. The pauses that prepared me.

Sometimes surrender doesn't look like open hands—it looks like tear-stained ones. It's choosing to trust that even when it doesn't *feel* good, God is still working it *for* good.

Because when our plans fall apart, His are just beginning.

I've learned that we always have two choices:

We can fight Him—dig our heels in, resist His timing, and grow bitter in the process.

Or we can surrender—release the illusion of control and allow peace to take its place.

Those who fight usually end up frustrated, cynical, and convinced that God somehow missed their turn. But those who surrender? They start to see beauty right where they are.

Because surrender isn't losing. It's aligning.

It's trading the exhausting burden of managing every outcome for the freedom of trusting the One who already knows how it all ends.

When Jesus prayed, "Not my will, but Yours be done," it wasn't weakness; it was the ultimate act of strength. The Son of God modeled what it means to trust a Father who sees the whole picture, even when the moment hurts.

So if life looks nothing like you planned right now—if you're standing in a version of your story that feels foreign or unfinished—take heart. You're not off course. You're just in the part where His plan is unfolding.

And one day, you'll look back and realize: It may not have gone the way you wanted, but it became something more beautiful than you could've written yourself.

Prayer:

Lord, thank You that Your plans are better than mine, even when I don't understand them. Help me to surrender what I thought life would look like and trust that what You're building is far greater. When I'm tempted to fight for control, remind me that peace lives on the other side of surrender. Amen.

DAY 39

Obedience Over Outcome

"To obey is better than sacrifice." — *1 Samuel 15:22*

I've spent a lot of time over the last couple of years talking about my *Formula for Fulfillment*:

Who + Why + How = Fulfillment

When I first wrote it, it wasn't Christ-centered (at least not intentionally). I thought fulfillment came from understanding *who* we are, *why* we're here, and *how* we live it out.

And while that's true, God's been showing me a deeper version of that formula—His version.

Our *who* isn't something we define; it's who we are *in Him*.

Our *why* isn't about personal purpose; it's about *His plan*.

And our *how*? That comes through *His promise*—and our obedience to them.

That last part—the obedience—is where things get tricky. Because obedience rarely comes with a preview.

Sometimes God doesn't reveal the *why* up front. He just says, "Take the step," and trusts that you'll move even when the map isn't clear.

And if you're anything like me, that's not easy.

I like knowing what's next. I like strategy and direction and five-year plans. But walking with God means surrendering the outcome and choosing obedience instead—even when it doesn't make sense.

There have been so many moments in my journey, especially as I've stepped into ministry, where I've had to obey before understanding.

Before clarity.

Before confirmation.

Sometimes He calls you to write the book before you know who will read it.

Sometimes He nudges you to step away from something good so He can make room for something *God*.

Sometimes He asks you to stay still when your instinct is to sprint ahead.

But that's the beauty of obedience—it's the "how" that unlocks everything else.

When you walk in obedience, even the unseen steps are sacred. You start to realize that God's measuring stick isn't *results*—it's *faithfulness*. He's not asking you to prove yourself. He's asking you to *trust* Him.

And the amazing thing?

When you do—when you take that step of faith without demanding all the answers—He always unfolds the *why* in His timing.

So if you're standing on the edge of something new, feeling unsure, take heart. You don't have to understand it all to take the next step. You just have to trust the One who does.

Because the win isn't in the outcome, it's in the obedience.

Prayer:

Lord, thank You for reminding me that You care more about my faithfulness than my performance. When I don't understand what You're doing, help me to obey anyway—to take the next step in faith, knowing You'll unfold the plan in Your perfect timing. Teach me to value obedience over outcome, and to find peace in trusting You with the rest. Amen.

DAY 40

The Potter's Hands

> "Yet you, Lord, are our Father. We are the clay, you are the potter; we are all the work of your hand." — *Isaiah 64:8*

I've actually done pottery before—and let me tell you, it's not the calm, peaceful experience people make it out to be. It's messy, unpredictable, and a whole lot harder to control than you'd expect.

And that's kind of how life feels when God starts shaping us, isn't it? We're on the wheel, things are spinning, and even when we think we know what He's making—He's over there crafting something completely different.

Now, if I had any say in how I was being shaped, I'd have requested a smaller waist and a higher, rounder booty ... but apparently, the Potter doesn't take custom orders.

Because God isn't interested in shaping what looks good—He's shaping what *lasts*.

There have been so many times in my life where I've felt His hands pressing in—molding, stretching, and smoothing areas I didn't want retouched. Those were the seasons that hurt the most, the ones that humbled me and stripped me of the illusion of control. I used to think He was undoing me, but I've learned He was really remaking me.

See, the Potter knows exactly what He's doing. When the clay starts to wobble, He doesn't toss it aside—He steadies it. When it collapses, He doesn't walk away—He gathers it back up and starts again. And when it's finally ready, He places it in the fire—not to destroy it, but to strengthen it.

That part, the fire? That's where the real growth happens. The same heat that could crack us without His care is what solidifies us when He's holding us.

So if you're in a season right now that feels like pressure—if you can't see the purpose, or it feels like life keeps reshaping you just when you thought you were "done" —you're not being ruined; you're being refined.

The Potter's process is never random. Every press, every pause, every fire serves a purpose. And one day, you'll look back and see His fingerprints all over your life—proof that even in the spinning, you were never out of His hands.

Prayer:

Lord, thank You for shaping me with purpose, even when it's uncomfortable. When I feel the pressure or the heat, remind me that I'm not being broken—I'm being built. Help me to trust Your hands, surrender to Your process, and see beauty in the way You're molding my life. Amen.

DAY 41

His Plan: The Body He Built for Purpose

> *"Do you not know that your bodies are temples of the Holy Spirit ... You are not your own; you were bought at a price." — 1 Corinthians 6:19–20*

I know this verse could be used to guilt people into green smoothies and extra squats—and listen, I love a good Pure Barre moment and a green juice when I'm feeling fancy, but let's be clear: This isn't about kale or cardio. It's about calling.

Because if we're honest, some of us (hi, it's me) have spent years believing our body was a problem to manage, not a purpose to carry.

I have had seasons where I stood in front of the mirror and thought, *"Lord, You sure You picked the right place to put Your Spirit? Because this ... this does not feel like a temple. This feels like maybe a storage unit. A well-loved one. One with late fees."*

I've grabbed at my stomach, criticized my thighs, replayed photos and said things about myself I wouldn't say to a stranger on the internet (and you know how bold people get on the internet).

There were years I treated my body like a before-and-after project that never quite made it to the "after." I was convinced God would use me *more* once I dropped the weight, tightened things up, or magically woke up one morning looking like I actually enjoyed long-distance running.

But then God (in the way only He does) whispered to my heart:

"I didn't wait for you to be flawless before I filled you. Why are you waiting to feel flawless before you let Me use you?"

Your body—the one that has carried babies or carried grief, that has gained weight in survival seasons or lost weight in stressful ones, the one that wakes up tired but still shows up ... that body is the exact one God chose to hold His Spirit.

He didn't ask you to be a sculpted statue. He asked you to be a willing vessel.

And vessels are not admired for their shape—they are honored for what they *carry.*

God's plan was never about having an "after" photo. It was never about finally being enough. It was always about Him being enough in you, through you, and with you—in the exact body you're living in today.

So whether you're lifting weights, lifting groceries, or lifting prayers you barely have the strength to whisper—He has purpose in every move you make, because He made you on purpose, for purpose.

Prayer:

God, thank You for this body—not because it is perfect, but because it is Yours. Teach me to honor it as a vessel You designed with intention, not as a project to constantly fix. Release me from comparison, criticism, and shame. Help me use this body to love, to serve, and to live out the purpose You placed inside me. Remind me that my worth is not measured by mirrors, photos, or numbers, but by Your plan and Your presence within me. Amen.

DAY 42

You Matter Here

> "And who knows but that you have come to your royal position for such a time as this?" — *Esther 4:14*

When most people think of this verse, they picture Esther—crown on her head, courage in her heart, standing in the palace with purpose written all over her life.

But what about when your "palace" looks more like a laundry room? Or an office cubicle? Or a season you never planned on being in?

Years ago, during the recession, I was laid off from my admin role in new construction. We had a young family, and I needed to roll up my sleeves and figure something out fast. That's when I started cleaning houses for a living.

It was good work—honest work—and I was good at it. There was satisfaction in seeing a home sparkle, in knowing I'd created a little peace for someone else's day. But if I'm honest, there were also moments I'd look around and think, *"Is this it, God? Is this what You had in mind for me?"*

Because from where I stood—sweaty, tired, surrounded by cleaning supplies—it didn't look like "purpose." It looked like survival.

But looking back now, I can see it so clearly. I was in ministry even then.

Every home I entered was a chance to serve others—to create comfort, to bring peace, to pour love into spaces that sometimes held chaos. It was humble work, but it was holy work, too. God wasn't punishing me with that season; He was *preparing* me in it.

That time taught me humility, discipline, and pride in doing good work—no matter what kind of work it was. It taught me that "calling" doesn't always come with a stage or a spotlight. Sometimes it comes with a mop and a prayer.

We like to think purpose lives in our dream job or the next big opportunity, but purpose is wherever God plants you. You don't have to wait until you "arrive" somewhere to matter—you already do.

You matter in your workplace.

You matter in your home.

You matter in your friendships, your community, your quiet faithfulness that no one else sees.

Like Esther, you've been positioned for purpose—but unlike her, your palace might not look grand. That doesn't make your role any less divine.

So if you're in a season that feels small, unseen, or far from where you thought you'd be, hold this close: God hasn't misplaced you. He's *positioned* you.

Every room you walk into—no matter how ordinary—is holy ground when you carry His love there.

You matter here. Right here. For such a time as this.

Prayer:

Lord, thank You for reminding me that I don't have to wait for a different title, season, or place to have purpose. Help me to see Your hand in my current circumstances and use my life—wherever I am—to bring comfort, kindness, and light to others. Let me serve You with joy in every season, knowing that I matter here, right where You've placed me. Amen.

DAY 43

Calling Ground

> "Whatever you do, work at it with all your heart, as working for the Lord, not for human masters." — *Colossians 3:23*

For most of my career, my world has revolved around *lead conversion*. That's the language of new home sales—turning interest into commitment, browsers into buyers. And to be fair, I've gotten pretty gosh dang good at it.

But recently, God gave me a revelation that stopped me in my tracks:

I've built a career on lead conversion ... but what He's really called me to is *life conversion*.

Now before you get the wrong idea, I'm not saying there's anything wrong with what I do—I love my work. I love the people, the homes, the process of helping families find a place to belong. But when I started reflecting on what truly matters, I realized how easy it is to get caught up in producing results instead of pursuing holy relationship.

I can't even begin to count the number of leads I've assisted in converting.

The promotions.

The awards.

The achievements that stretch for miles on my résumé.

But when I ask myself, *How many lives have I helped convert?*

How many people have seen Jesus through the way I lead, serve, and love? —the number feels painfully small.

That's when it hit me: My career was never just a job. It was—and is—my *calling ground*.

The marketplace is my ministry.

God didn't put me in the homebuilding industry by accident. He placed me there so I could help build more than houses—so I could help build people. My office, my model homes, the sales centers, the construction sites—that's my pulpit. That's where I get to live out my faith, not by preaching sermons, but by showing up with integrity, empathy, and love.

You don't have to stand at a pulpit to preach. Sometimes your platform is a boardroom, a job site, a kitchen table, or a cubicle that smells faintly of burnt coffee. Wherever you are—*that's* your calling ground.

Because every environment is holy ground when you bring the Holy Spirit with you.

So whether you're signing contracts, raising kids, managing projects, teaching classes, or running a business—your work is worship when it's done with Him and for Him.

And here's the beautiful part: God isn't keeping score of your sales, promotions, or awards. He's looking at your impact. How many lives have you touched? How many hearts have you encouraged? How many people have seen a glimpse of Him because of how you showed up today?

If that question stings a little, you're not alone. It did for me too. But it also lit a fire in me—a desire to spend the rest of my life shifting my focus from *leads to lives*. From success to significance.

Because at the end of the day, the best conversion we'll ever be part of isn't found in spreadsheets or sales reports—it's found in the people whose lives are changed because we were willing to be a light where God placed us.

So go ahead—work hard, love people, and do what you do *with all your heart*. Just remember: Your career isn't just your job. It's your calling ground.

Prayer:

Lord, thank You for giving me purpose right where I am. Help me to see my workplace as more than a job—as a mission field. Teach me to bring Your love into every conversation, every decision, every ordinary moment. May the work of my hands point people toward You, and may my life be a reflection of the One I work for. Amen.

DAY 44

There's a Plan for You, Too

"The Lord will fulfill His purpose for me." — Psalm 138:8

It's easy to believe that God has big plans for other people—the speakers, the writers, the missionaries, the "out-loud" kinds of people who seem to live on fire for their calling. But when it comes to our own story, we tend to think maybe we were just assigned the supporting role.

I've felt that way before. Maybe you have too.

But I want to tell you about my friend Laura.

Laura is one of those people you can't help but love. She's creative, sharp, funny, wildly thoughtful—and she's got the kind of curly hair that deserves its own fan club. She's the person who shows up with joy, cheers on others with her whole heart, and somehow makes everyone around her feel a little brighter.

When I was preparing for my TEDx Talk on fulfillment, I sent out a survey to better understand how people defined and experienced it. Hundreds of responses came in, full of hope, struggle, and wisdom. But one answer stopped me in my tracks.

When asked if fulfillment felt achievable in the future, only one person said *no*.

That person was Laura.

Her response broke my heart a little. She wrote, *"I just wonder if I lack the motivation to work on myself enough to get there. Work motivation is easy, but self-improvement is hard. At this moment, I don't see how that changes."*

She also shared that she's wired to achieve—to push, to do more, to reach the next goal. And even when she got there, it never felt like enough. She said, *"Once X happens, I'll be happy."* But X would come and go, and the satisfaction never stuck.

Can I just say—same, girl, same.

It's that achiever's trap so many of us fall into: chasing fulfillment like it's something we can earn. And when we can't grab hold of it, we start to think maybe God's plan skipped over us.

But then, something shifted for Laura.

Not long ago, she reached out to tell me that she had discovered her "who." She said, *"I've known this about myself for a while, but it finally clicked. I'm a cheerleader for good—good people, good causes, good brands. I'm wired to wave the flag for others and remind them how amazing they are. It's who I am."*

And I thought—*yes, you are.*

She's the biggest cheerleader I know. She shows up for people again and again, not because it earns her anything, but because that's what she was *created* to do. She was designed to encourage, to amplify, to champion others.

Her purpose isn't small—it's sacred.

Laura's story reminds me of something so important: Purpose isn't ranked. It's assigned.

We look at others and think, *"God's really doing something through her."* But friend, He's doing something through *you* too. It might look different—maybe quieter, maybe slower, maybe without the stage lights—but it's no less divine.

God doesn't hand out background roles. Every part in His story matters.

You're not the understudy in someone else's calling. You're the leading role in yours.

And here's the truth—you don't have to *find* your purpose as much as you have to *live* it. It's already in you. In the way you love people. In the way you show up when no one's watching. In the way you cheer for others even when your own season feels uncertain.

Because the Lord *will* fulfill His purpose for you. Not *might*. Not *if you work hard enough*. He *will*.

So if you're doubting your worth or wondering if you're doing enough, remember this: You were never meant to do it all—you were meant to do *yours*.

And that? That's more than enough.

Prayer:

Lord, thank You for reminding me that You don't create extras—You create originals. Help me stop comparing my calling to someone else's and instead walk confidently in the purpose You've written just for me. When I feel unseen or unsure, whisper this truth back to me: I matter. I'm called. And You have a plan for me, too. Amen.

DAY 45

Listening for the Whisper

"And after the fire came a gentle whisper." — 1 Kings 19:11–12

I'll be the first to admit it—I like clarity.

Give me a plan, a timeline, a color-coded spreadsheet of what's next, and I'm good to go.

Or even better, a detailed email from Heaven titled *"Here's the Plan."* But God doesn't usually work that way, does He?

He rarely gives us the full plan up front. Most of the time, He just gives us His voice—and not a booming, unmistakable one either. A whisper. A soft, steady nudge that cuts through the noise if (and only if) we're quiet long enough to hear it.

The truth is, I haven't always been great at quiet. I'm a thinker, a planner, a doer—I fill my days and my head with words, noise, and motion. And yet, I've learned that some of the most defining moments of my faith haven't come through the loud or the obvious. They've come in the stillness.

After speaking at an event recently, a woman waited to talk with me afterward. She told me she leads a small women's group and that they'd been having a discussion about hearing God's voice—how to tell when it's really Him and not just our own thoughts. Then she asked, *"How do you know when you hear God's voice?"*

I'll be honest, my first thought was, *"Why is she asking me that?"*

But her question stuck with me long after that conversation. Because the truth is, we all wonder that, don't we?

How do we know it's *Him*?

1 Kings tells the story of Elijah waiting to hear from God. He expected a dramatic entrance—a powerful wind, an earthquake, a fire. But God wasn't in any of those. He came in the whisper.

And that's how He still speaks.

We often expect God's voice to be loud or unmistakable—but more often than not, it's subtle. It's a stirring in your spirit, a verse that lingers, a peace that doesn't make sense, a conviction wrapped in kindness.

Here's how I've learned to recognize it: God's voice never rushes, shames, or confuses you. It doesn't sound like anxiety or guilt. His voice is steady, patient, gentle—and it always aligns with His Word.

When He speaks, it brings peace, even when it challenges you. It draws you closer, not further away.

Maybe that's why He whispers—because a whisper means you have to lean in close to hear it.

So if you're wondering whether God is speaking to you, the answer is yes. He is. The real question is: Are you close enough, quiet enough, still enough to hear Him?

He's not waiting to shout. He's waiting for you to lean in.

Prayer:

Lord, help me slow down and listen for You. Tune my heart to recognize Your voice—the one that brings peace, not pressure; truth, not turmoil. When the noise of life grows loud, help me lean in close to Your whisper and follow where You lead. Amen.

DAY 46

Bloom Where You're Planted

> "But blessed is the one who trusts in the Lord, whose confidence is in him. They will be like a tree planted by the water that sends out its roots by the stream. It does not fear when heat comes; its leaves are always green. It has no worries in a year of drought and never fails to bear fruit." — *Jeremiah 17:7–8*

Let's be real for a second—sometimes "bloom where you're planted" sounds a lot prettier than it feels.

Because some seasons don't feel like blooming. They feel like surviving.

Or more honestly? Like *barely hanging on to your sanity while trying not to stab your eyeballs out with a fork.*

A few years back, after serving as a sales leader for a major builder in my market, I made the tough decision to leave. It wasn't because I didn't love the people—I did. But there was a level of toxicity I had allowed for too long, and it was time to go.

Not long after, I landed a new opportunity with a lending company that had a real estate arm. It happened quickly, and I was grateful. I thought, *Okay, God, this must be where You're leading me next.*

Except ... no.

That job? Whew. It was a doozy.

Let's just say I traded one toxic environment for another—only this one came with a side of chaos and confusion that had me praying for patience on an hourly basis. Most days, I wanted to stab my eyeballs out with a fork. (Kidding ... mostly.)

But looking back now, I can see it so clearly: That season was a stepping stone. A necessary part of the plan.

Because just weeks into that fork-eye-stabbing season, I got a call. My now company—the one that's been the best environment, the healthiest culture, the biggest blessing of my professional life—reached out. At the time, they weren't ready to hire for a leadership position, but the conversations began. And a few months later, the door opened wide.

Had I skipped the in-between season, I wouldn't have been ready. My heart needed to heal. My boundaries needed to strengthen. My leadership needed refining.

That hard, uncomfortable, "Why am I here" job was actually God's holding pattern—the waiting room before the breakthrough.

Here's the thing about blooming where you're planted:

It doesn't mean pretending every season is wonderful.

It means trusting that *every season is working toward something wonderful.*

God doesn't waste your waiting.

He doesn't misplace your purpose.

And He never plants you without intention.

So if you're in a job, relationship, or season right now that feels like it's testing your patience more than it's growing your peace—hang in there. The same God who planted you there will carry you through it and move you when it's time.

You're not stuck. You're being shaped.

And one day, you'll look back and realize—you bloomed anyway.

Prayer:
Lord, thank You for the reminder that even when the soil feels dry and the environment feels hard, You are still growing something good in me. Help me to stay faithful where You've placed me, to trust Your timing, and to keep blooming—even in the in-between. Amen.

DAY 47

The Shepherd's Voice

"My sheep listen to my voice; I know them, and they follow me." — John 10:27

You know how you can be in a crowded room, ten different conversations going at once, and still somehow hear your best friend's voice above the noise? You don't even have to see her—you just *know*.

That's what it's like to know God's voice.

It's not about volume. It's about familiarity.

When Jesus said, "My sheep listen to My voice," He wasn't talking about us suddenly hearing an audible voice from Heaven every time we need direction. (Though let's be honest—that would make life easier.)

He was talking about relationship—the kind that builds through time, trust, and consistency.

The more time you spend with Him, the easier it is to recognize His voice when He speaks.

When you've read His Word, you know what truth sounds like.

When you've prayed and wrestled and waited with Him, you know what peace feels like.

When you've seen His faithfulness show up again and again, you know when something aligns with His heart—and when it doesn't.

That's the beauty of walking with the Shepherd.

You don't have to panic over every decision, wondering if you'll "miss" His voice. He's not trying to trick you. He's not whispering riddles and hoping you guess right.

He wants to be known.

And the more familiar you become with His voice, the easier it is to tell when something *isn't* Him. The enemy can imitate tone but not truth. God's voice will never contradict His Word. It won't stir anxiety or shame. It won't rush you or confuse you. His voice will always lead you toward peace, humility, and love.

Here's a little confession: I used to think I needed big, flashing signs to know what God wanted from me. But now? I've learned to recognize the quiet nudge, the verse that won't leave my heart, the conversation that hits a little too close to coincidence. Those moments—that's Him.

And when you know His voice, you start to trust His leading, even when you can't see the full map.

So, if you're wondering how to hear God more clearly, start here:

Open your Bible.

Talk to Him often.

Listen more than you speak.

Because His voice isn't distant—it's devoted. And once you know it, you'll never mistake it again.

Prayer:

Lord, thank You for being a Shepherd who speaks, leads, and knows me by name. Help me to recognize Your voice above all others—the one that brings peace, not panic; clarity, not confusion. Tune my heart to hear You in the quiet and to follow You with confidence. Amen.

DAY 48

When You Feel Behind

"Though it linger, wait for it; it will certainly come and will not delay." — Habakkuk 2:3

You ever feel like God accidentally left you on "pause"?

Like everyone else got the divine green light—new jobs, dream houses, purpose-finding, glowing-skin seasons—and you're just over here waiting for your turn, staring at the sky like, *"Hey, Lord ... did You forget to hit play on me?"*

Yeah. Been there.

I was hitting milestones, checking boxes, doing all the things that should have felt like "moving forward." But deep down, something felt ... off. Like I was playing the right notes in the wrong song.

There was this tug—a calling toward *something different*.

But instead of leaping into it, I froze.

I got stuck in what I call the "holy holding pattern."

It's that phase where you know God's stirring something new, but instead of taking a brave step, you binge-clean your pantry, overanalyze everything, and convince yourself that maybe the timing's just *off*. (Spoiler: it's usually fear wearing a very convincing disguise.)

So while I was stuck, I watched others moving—fast.

Launching things. Leading things. Living out their "God-sized dreams." And I was thrilled for them ... while simultaneously asking

Jesus, *"Um, did You misplace my assignment folder? Maybe check the bottom of Gabriel's inbox?"*

It's funny now, but in the moment, I felt behind—like everyone else was sprinting toward purpose while I was out here tying my shoes.

But here's what I've learned since: God's timeline isn't like ours. He's not watching a clock. He's watching your *character.*

Sometimes the waiting isn't punishment; it's preparation.

Sometimes being "stuck" is actually being *set apart.*

That restless feeling you have? That's not failure—it's growth.

It's God saying, *"I'm not done with this version of you yet."*

Habakkuk 2:3 reminds us that, *"Though it linger, wait for it; it will certainly come and will not delay."* Translation: It might feel late to you, but it's *right on time* for Him.

So if you're feeling behind—take heart.

You're not lagging; you're being aligned.

You're not delayed; you're being developed.

And while you're over there panicking about your pace, God's up there grinning like, *"Sweet girl, we're not even late."*

So unclench your jaw, stop refreshing the tracking number on your calling, and trust that when it's time, you won't miss it.

He's got you on schedule. Promise.

Prayer:

Lord, thank You for reminding me that Your timing doesn't run on my calendar. When I start to feel behind, help me see the beauty in becoming, not rushing. Teach me to trust that You're not making me wait to punish me, but to prepare me. And maybe, just maybe, help me stop checking the spiritual clock every five minutes. Amen

DAY 49

Ministry Without a Microphone

> "Let your light shine before others, that they may see your good deeds and glorify your Father in heaven." — *Matthew 5:16*

Okay, between you and me—I have to keep it real.

For years (and when I say years, I mean *years*), God kept putting ministry on my heart ... and I hated it.

There, I said it.

I know, that sounds terrible. But it's true.

I didn't understand it. I didn't *want* it. I mean, me? In ministry? Why?

I asked Him that question so many times that I'm sure Heaven rolled its eyes.

So, naturally, I did what any good, obedient Christian woman does when faced with divine instruction—I ignored it.

But ministry has this funny way of boomeranging back around. I'd push it away for a while, and just when I thought, *"Okay, maybe that phase is over,"* it would show right back up. Louder. Clearer. More convicting.

The closer I got to God's purpose, the stronger the conviction became.

But so did my resistance.

See, when I thought of "ministry," I pictured the Bible-totin',

Scripture-quotin', holy-rollin' Sunday saints—the ones who could recite Leviticus before breakfast and make you feel a guilty conviction about how you buttered your toast. And, don't get me wrong, those folks are wonderful, but that's just not me.

Meanwhile, I'm over here being the sin-sittin', delivery-doubtin', messy-mission kind of Jesus follower.

So yeah, I used to wonder how exactly *this* girl was supposed to fit into *that* kind of ministry.

I didn't want to preach *at* people. I wanted to love people *to* Jesus. People like me.

But I couldn't see how I fit into that world.

Until one day, I shared all this with my dear friend, Hope.

(And can we just take a second to appreciate how poetic it is that God used someone literally named *Hope* to help me see this differently?)

She listened to me go on and on about how unqualified I felt—how ministry didn't feel like "my lane."

Then she said, "Amy, I'm not surprised by this calling. Don't you realize ... you're already in ministry?"

And *bam*.

That one hit me square in the chest.

Because she was right. I needed to stop asking "why me?" And start saying "use me." Because he could, and he wanted to—right where I was.

It wasn't about standing behind a pulpit. It was about standing beside people.

It wasn't about having a platform—it was about having purpose.

It wasn't about preaching sermons—it was about living one.

Ministry isn't a title. It's a posture.

Every time you show kindness when you could have stayed silent—that's ministry.

Every time you forgive when you had every right not to—that's ministry.

Every time you cheer someone on, love them through their mess, or choose grace over gossip—that's ministry.

You don't need a microphone to make Kingdom noise.

So if you've ever felt unqualified or unsure about how God could use you, hear me: You are already being used. You already are.

In your office. In your home. In the carpool line. At the grocery store.

Every space you walk into is your mission field.

You don't have to *look* like ministry to *live* it.

So keep showing up. Keep shining your light. Keep doing the good work that glorifies Him—not by performance, but by presence.

Because when your life reflects Jesus, you're preaching the loudest kind of sermon there is.

Prayer:

Lord, thank You for reminding me that ministry isn't about microphones—it's about moments. Help me see every interaction as a chance to reflect Your love. Use my words, my work, and even my imperfections to point people to You. Let my life be the sermon that someone else needs to hear today. Amen.

DAY 50

Divine Appointments

> "Many are the plans in a person's heart, but it is the Lord's purpose that prevails." — *Proverbs 19:21*

You know those days when you wake up with a perfectly planned to-do list, color-coded and organized, and then God looks at it and says, "Aww, that's cute"?

Yeah. Those are what I like to call *divine appointment days*.

Because as much as I love a plan (and you know I do), God loves a good interruption.

And honestly? Some of the most meaningful moments in my life weren't scheduled, structured, or even remotely on my radar. They showed up disguised as interruptions—and ended up being invitations.

One of my favorite examples of this is my friend Cassy.

If you've been around me long enough, you've heard me talk about her before. Cassy is what I like to call "a love hurricane." She loves people big, bold, and loud—the kind of love you can't outrun. And, she has the best Cassy-isms.

One time, we were talking about difficult people—you know, the ones that test your patience *and* your salvation—and Cassy said something I'll never forget.

She said, "When someone's hard to love, I just make it my mission to love 'em down®." (There is actually a whole chapter devoted to this subject in her book "Unapologetic")

Love. Them. Down.

She said it so simply, like it was no big deal. But that's Cassy. She doesn't just talk about loving people—she *does it*. Whether they're prickly, guarded, or downright unpleasant, she shows up and loves them until the walls come down. She believes everyone was placed in her path for a purpose—they are all divine appointments so she treats them as such. Both good and bad.

You see, Cassy's way of life is to love all, accept all, and we all know that when we do that we hope to receive it back in return, but it doesn't always work that way. Sometimes people are put in our path to receive the love we have, not to give it. And that can feel hard for us "big lovers."

But Cassy, she has gotten really good at this. She just "loves 'em down" anyway.

That's ministry. That's divine appointment living.

See, divine appointments aren't usually neat or convenient.

They rarely happen when your hair's washed or your schedule's open. They happen in grocery store lines, text messages, and chance encounters that feel random—until you realize God planned them all along.

Sometimes the person who interrupts your day is the person God meant for you to notice all along.

Proverbs 19:21 reminds us, *"Many are the plans in a person's heart, but it is the Lord's purpose that prevails."* Translation: You can plan your day all you want, but God might just reroute it for something way more important.

So when life doesn't go as planned—when someone needs you, when you get delayed, when your meeting runs long—take a breath. It might not be a disruption. It might be a divine assignment.

And if you're ever unsure of how to handle that unexpected moment, just remember Cassy's wisdom—love 'em down®.

Because sometimes the biggest Kingdom impact happens in the smallest, most inconvenient moments.

Prayer:

Lord, help me slow down enough to see the people You place in my path today. When my plans are interrupted, remind me that Your purpose is always greater than my schedule. Give me a heart like Cassy's—one that loves people down until they see You through me. Amen.

DAY 51

Clearing the Clutter

> "Let us throw off everything that hinders and the sin that so easily entangles." — *Hebrews 12:1*

All right, confession time.

I can be what you might call a *sin sitter*.

You know what I mean—the kind of person who doesn't just stumble into sin but *sets up camp* in it.

When I fall into something I know I shouldn't be doing, I don't always bounce right back up with a halo and a worship playlist. Nope. I'll sit right there in it—wrapped up like it's a cozy blanket. I'll hunker down, get comfortable, and settle in for a few days ... or weeks.

And here's the wild part: I know exactly what I'm doing.

Like, fully aware. Consciously choosing.

I've even had conversations with God about it—and y'all, they go something like this:

"Okay, Jesus ... I know this is wrong. Like, I'm not even going to pretend I don't know. But I'm just going to need You to be my dog right now—walk with me through this, okay? And maybe, if You could, just protect me while I make this really bad choice?"

Wild, right?

And yet—He does. He stays. He protects. Even when I'm being a total mess.

But here's the thing I've learned the hard way:

God's grace doesn't mean His permission.

He loves us *through* our sin, yes, but He also loves us *too much* to let us stay there.

Those "comfort sins"—the habits, the mindsets, the coping mechanisms we keep going back to—they might feel safe for a minute, but really, they're clutter. They take up space where peace, joy, and purpose are supposed to live.

And if I'm being honest, I know there are some sins, some patterns, some people, that I can't take with me into my next season. Not if I truly want to step into what God's calling me to do.

Sometimes it's not that we're waiting on God to move—it's that He's waiting on us to make room.

The verse says, *"Throw off everything that hinders and the sin that so easily entangles."*

It's not a gentle suggestion; it's a full-on spiritual declutter.

God can't pour fresh purpose into a heart that's packed with old junk.

So maybe it's time to do a little cleaning. To stop sitting in the sin and start standing in the freedom He's already given us.

Because what He has next for you—it's too good to miss because you're tangled up in what's meant to be left behind.

So, if you're like me and you've been "sin sittin'" for a bit—pull off those blankets, take a deep breath, and hand them over. He's got something better waiting.

Prayer:

Lord, thank You for loving me even when I'm wrapped up in my mess. Help me see the clutter I've been clinging to and give me the courage to let it go. Clear out what's hindering my heart so I can step freely into the purpose You've prepared for me. Amen.

DAY 52

Out With the Old

> "Therefore, if anyone is in Christ, the new creation has come: The old has gone, the new is here!" — *2 Corinthians 5:17*

You know that feeling when your closet is overflowing, but you still tell yourself, "I have nothing to wear"?

Yeah. That's what it's like trying to step into a new season while dragging all your old stuff with you.

At some point, you've got to let go of the jeans that don't fit—and the junk that doesn't either.

Spiritually, emotionally, even relationally—I've had a few "closet cleanouts" with God. And let me tell you, He doesn't just Marie Kondo your life; He *renovates* it.

There have been things, people, and patterns I've tried to hold on to way past their expiration date. Because even when something isn't good for us anymore, it's still familiar, and familiar feels safe.

But God isn't calling us to stay comfortable. He's calling us to be *changed*.

And change means release.

There was a season where God made it very clear that I needed to let go of something I thought I needed, something I had built part of my identity around. And to be honest, I fought Him on it. Hard. I wanted His blessing without the surrender.

But you can't step into your new story if you're still clinging to the old chapter.

When I finally let go, it hurt. It felt like loss. But what I didn't realize was that God wasn't taking something *from* me—He was making room to give something *to* me.

That's how healing works. It usually starts with deleting what no longer fits.

Old habits. Old labels. Old lies.

That version of you served its purpose—but it can't carry the new one.

The verse says, "The old has gone, the new is here."

Not "the old is hanging around just in case we need it later." Gone. Done. Over.

Because you are a new creation.

Not an upgraded model—a *whole new thing.*

So maybe it's time to hit "unsubscribe" on the shame, the doubt, the comfort zone, and the situations that don't line up with where He's taking you.

You're not who you were—and thank God for that.

The new is here.

And it looks good on you.

Prayer:

Lord, thank You for making me new. Show me what I need to release so I can walk freely into what You're building next. Give me courage to let go of what's familiar and confidence to trust that the new You're calling me into is better, because it's from You. Amen.

DAY 53

Unfinished and Unforgotten

> "He who began a good work in you will carry it on to completion." — *Philippians 1:6*

If I'm being totally honest, I love a good finished product. Crossing something off my to-do list is my love language.

I like the freshly painted room, the organized closet, the wrapped-up project. I'm a sucker for a *"before and after."*

But do you know what I *don't* like?

The *during*.

That awkward, messy middle where everything looks worse before it looks better—paint cans everywhere, dust flying, no clear sign that this will ever turn into something pretty.

Spiritually speaking, that's where I find myself more often than not—right smack in the middle of a divine renovation.

God's still working, but it doesn't always *look* like it.

There are seasons when the progress feels invisible. You pray, you show up, you keep doing the "right" things ... and it still feels like you're walking in circles. The goals aren't done, the healing isn't complete, the calling isn't clear, and patience is running on fumes.

That's when the enemy likes to whisper, *"See? God forgot about you."*

But Philippians 1:6 shuts that lie down quick: *"He who began a good work in you will carry it on to completion."*

That means He doesn't start what He won't finish.

And He doesn't misplace His people halfway through the process.

You're not behind—you're *becoming*.

You're not forgotten—you're *forming*.

God isn't sitting in Heaven looking at you thinking, *"Wow, she was off to such a good start. Too bad she fizzled out."*

No. He's saying, *"I'm still working on her. This chapter's just not done yet."*

If you've ever watched a puzzle being built, it's chaotic until the final piece snaps in. From above, the Creator already sees the full picture. You just see the scattered pieces.

So today, if you're feeling half-finished, hold tight.

The Artist hasn't put the brush down.

Your story is still being written.

And when it's complete, it's going to make sense in a way it never could in the middle.

Because unfinished doesn't mean forgotten.

It just means *He's still working*.

Prayer:

Lord, thank You that You never leave projects—or people—half done. When I can't see progress, remind me You're still painting the picture. Give me patience in the process and faith to trust that what You started, You will finish. Amen.

DAY 54

The Worthy Work

> "Live a life worthy of the calling you have received." — *Ephesians 4:1*

If I'm being honest, this verse used to stress me out.

Live a life worthy of the calling you have received.

Like, okay Paul—no pressure, right?

Because if you're anything like me, your first thought might be, *"Worthy? Me? Have you met me?"*

I've had plenty of moments where I've felt wildly unqualified for the things God was calling me to do. Honestly, my résumé doesn't exactly scream "divine spokesperson." I'm more of the *sin-sittin', grace-grabbin', messy-but-trying* type.

And yet—He called me anyway.

Because God doesn't call the qualified; He qualifies the called.

When He asks you to step into something bigger than yourself, it's not because He forgot your flaws, it's because He knows His power shines brighter *through* them.

It's funny ... we spend so much time waiting until we "feel ready" to walk in our purpose. But I don't think God's ever used someone who *felt* ready. He uses the willing ones. The brave-enough ones. The "Okay God, I don't get it, but I'll go anyway" ones.

When I first started speaking, I was a bundle of nerves and doubt. I kept wondering, *"Who am I to be on this stage? Who am I to teach anyone anything?"*

And I swear I could almost hear God laugh and whisper, *"Exactly. You're Mine. That's who."*

Your worthiness doesn't come from what you've done; it comes from Who called you.

And when you start to see your calling not as a burden but as a *privilege*, everything shifts.

It's not about proving yourself—it's about reflecting Him.

The "worthy work" isn't about being perfect at what you do; it's about being present where He's placed you.

You don't have to *earn* your calling. You just have to *live* it— with humility, confidence, and a whole lot of grace for yourself along the way.

So go ahead—walk boldly into the work He's entrusted to you.

Not because you have it all together, but because He does.

Prayer:

Lord, thank You for calling me even when I feel unqualified. Remind me that my worth isn't found in my perfection but in Your purpose. Help me walk boldly in my calling—with confidence, humility, and faith that You'll give me everything I need along the way. Amen.

DAY 55

Hearing His Direction

> "Trust in the Lord with all your heart ... and He will make your paths straight." — *Proverbs 3:5–6*

If you've ever tried to use your car's GPS in a sketchy signal zone, then you know the feeling of total chaos. You're cruising along, minding your business, and suddenly your GPS says, "Recalculating," right as you pass the only exit for ten miles.

That's me with God's direction sometimes.

I want a turn-by-turn voice command. I want clear signage and maybe even a holy traffic report while we're at it. But more often than not, God gives me ... silence.

Or a nudge.

Or a whisper that sounds an awful lot like, *"Trust Me."*

And trust doesn't always come easy for a planner like me. I'm the kind of person who likes to have the route mapped out, laminated, and possibly stored in a cute binder. But God isn't Google Maps. He's more like, "Start driving, I'll guide you as we go."

There have been seasons where I thought I was *so sure* of the next step. I'd prayed, made a plan, maybe even announced it (whoops) ... and then the plan completely unraveled. And I'd sit there confused, disappointed, and wondering, *Did I hear You wrong, God?*

But looking back, I can see it so clearly—He was protecting me. Redirecting me.

Because His "no" was actually a *not yet*.

And His silence wasn't absence—it was alignment.

Trust often comes *before* clarity.

We want the map first, but He gives us the next step.

When I finally started praying less for answers and more for awareness, I began to see His direction everywhere—through Scripture, through peace (or the lack of it), through wise friends, through that little gut feeling that wouldn't go away.

Sometimes the voice of God sounds like a whisper.

Sometimes it sounds like a door closing.

And sometimes it sounds like your own sigh of surrender

when you finally let go of your plan and follow His.

He doesn't just have a plan for you—He wants to *walk it with you*.

So if you're in a season where you can't see ten steps ahead, take the one step He's given you.

You don't need to see the whole road when you know Who's driving.

Prayer:

Lord, help me to trust You even when I can't see the way forward. Give me a listening heart that recognizes Your direction and a steady spirit that follows even when it doesn't make sense. Remind me that You don't just plan my path—you walk beside me every step of the way. Amen.

DAY 56

Purpose in the Pain

> "You intended to harm me, but God intended it for good ..." — *Genesis 50:20*

There are some people on this earth who just radiate Jesus. You know the kind—the ones who make you feel seen, safe, and somehow closer to Heaven just by standing next to them.

That's my friend Sarah.

If you've ever met her, you already know what I mean. She's what I like to call *heaven walking on earth*. She attracts believers, steady hearts, and lost souls alike—because her presence feels like peace.

Sarah's the kind of friend who picks up the phone on the first ring, prays with you mid-conversation, and somehow manages to make you laugh right after she's made you cry. She's my ear, my confidant, my barre buddy, and my person.

And she's been walking through a season that doesn't make sense.

In the past year, Sarah's faced loss, sickness in her family, health scares for her husband and parents, and—just to make sure the storm hit every corner—she's been grinding through a tough market professionally too. Any *one* of those things could take a person down. But she's facing them all at once.

And yet—her faith hasn't wavered.

Tonight, after barre class (because yes, we are those girls who stretch and then solve the world's problems in the parking lot), Sarah stood there with tears streaming down her face. The weight of everything finally spilled over. I listened as she whispered, "I know God's in this ... I just don't understand it yet."

That's the kind of faith that shakes Heaven.

Because real faith isn't loud. It's not all victory shouts and perfect peace. Sometimes it's the quiet surrender in the middle of the parking lot, mascara running, saying, "God, I trust You anyway."

Genesis 50:20 reminds us that what the enemy means for harm, God will use for good.

And sometimes, that "good" doesn't show up right away. It grows slowly, under the ashes.

I don't know what Sarah's story will look like when the dust settles—but I know this: God is already working through her pain. Her strength, her surrender, her steadfast heart—they're already ministering to others (like me).

That's the thing about pain—it often becomes our greatest platform for purpose.

Your scars, your tears, your "Why, God?" moments—they're not wasted. They're being woven into someone else's healing story.

If you're in the middle of your own painful season, hold onto this truth:

God doesn't waste wounds.

He's using every bit of it—

the loss, the fear, the fire—

to build something beautiful and unbreakable in you.

Prayer:

Lord, thank You for staying close in the pain. Help me trust that what I can't yet understand is still part of Your good plan. Use my hurt to help others find hope. Turn every scar into a story that points back to You. Amen.

DAY 57

The Refining Fire

"See, I have refined you, though not as silver; I have tested you in the furnace of affliction" — Isaiah 48:10

I don't know about you, but when I hear the word *fire,* my first thought isn't exactly "Yay, spiritual growth!"

Nope. My first thought is, *"Lord, please don't make me the one You're 'refining' right now."*

But here's the truth—refinement isn't punishment. It's preparation.

When gold is refined, it isn't destroyed. It's purified. The fire burns away the impurities that keep it from reflecting light. What's left behind is stronger, more radiant, and more valuable than before.

And that's exactly what God does with us.

The heat of life's trials—the heartbreaks, the waiting, the disappointments, the unexpected no's—they're not meant to break you down. They're meant to burn off what's been holding you back.

I think of all the times I've prayed for God to use me ... and then immediately asked Him to please not make it uncomfortable. (*As if those two things could coexist.*)

But God loves us too much to leave us unrefined. He knows the pride, control, and comfort we cling to so tightly can't go with us into the next chapter of our purpose. So He turns up the heat—not to harm us, but to free us.

Sometimes that "fire" looks like a door closing.

Sometimes it's a relationship ending.

Sometimes it's sitting in a season that doesn't make sense and thinking, *"I don't even recognize myself anymore."*

That's the refining process.

It's uncomfortable, it's holy, and it's where faith grows roots.

Because genuine faith isn't proven on the mountaintop—it's formed in the fire.

So if you're feeling the flames right now, take heart.

You're not being burned down. You're being made new.

You're not being punished. You're being purified.

And when the smoke clears, you'll see it—the shimmer of a stronger, braver, brighter you.

The fire didn't take you out. It brought you through.

Prayer:

Lord, thank You for loving me enough to refine me. When the heat feels too heavy, remind me that You're still holding me in Your hands. Burn away what no longer serves Your purpose and help me shine with a faith that's been tested—and proven true. Amen.

DAY 58

The Divine Cleanup Crew

> "Create in me a clean heart, O God, and renew a right spirit within me." — *Psalm 51:10*

If there's one thing I learned during my season of cleaning houses, it's that some messes take more than a quick wipe-down.

You can light all the candles you want, but there's no covering the smell of built-up neglect. Sometimes, you have to get down on your hands and knees, move the furniture, and scrub what no one else can see.

That's what God does with our hearts.

He's not afraid of the mess—He just wants permission to start the cleanup.

When I cleaned homes, I loved the feeling of walking out of a house knowing that every surface was shining again. But you know what? It always started with chaos—dust-covered surfaces, sticky floors, crumbs that seemed to multiply overnight. Before beauty came, there was work to do.

And that's exactly how God renovates our hearts.

He moves through the corners we've ignored—pride, bitterness, bad habits, guilt—and says, "Let's deal with this." It's not about shame. It's about freedom. He's not cleaning to condemn you; He's clearing space so His Spirit can move in.

Repentance isn't punishment—it's permission.

It's letting the Divine Cleanup Crew come in, roll up His sleeves, and make room for joy again.

David's prayer in Psalm 51 wasn't just about forgiveness. It was about *renewal*. He didn't ask for a "good enough" heart—he asked for a *clean* one. A heart that could breathe again, free from the clutter that was crowding God out.

So if it feels like He's rearranging your life, moving things around, or cleaning up some old corners, don't resist it. The dust is temporary, but the peace that follows is permanent.

Because every sweep of His hand is an act of love.

And when He's finished, you'll stand back and realize—He didn't just tidy you up. He transformed you.

Prayer:

Lord, thank You for loving me enough to clean up the parts of my life I've tried to hide. Help me to release what's cluttering my heart so You can fill it with what's holy. Make me new again, fresh and ready for whatever You're building next. Amen.

DAY 59

The Worth of His Plan

> "You are worth more than many sparrows." — *Matthew 10:29–31*

You know what I've realized? Self-doubt is sneaky. It doesn't always show up waving red flags and shouting, *"Hey! I'm insecurity!"* Sometimes, it hides behind really noble-sounding thoughts like:

"I just want to make sure I'm qualified."

"I don't want to mess this up."

"Maybe someone else could do this better."

Sound familiar? Yeah, me too.

If I had a dollar for every time I've questioned whether I'm worthy of what God's asked me to do, I could probably fund my own book tour—and buy a whole lot of Starbucks along the way.

Here's the thing though: God doesn't hand out assignments based on résumés. He gives them based on relationship.

And when He chose you (yes, *you*) for His plan, He already factored in your flaws, your fears, and your "Are you sure about this, Lord?" moments.

You weren't a backup pick or a "Well, she'll do for now" situation. You were the plan.

It's wild to think about, right? That the same God who hung the stars also looked at you and said, "Yep, she's the one for this."

But still, we question it. We look around at other people's lives—their highlight reels, their confidence, their seemingly flawless faith and we start believing the lie that maybe His plan for us was a little too big, or maybe we're not ready.

Let me lovingly say this: Stop shrinking to fit the lie.

You are worth every ounce of the purpose He's placed inside you. Not because of what you've achieved, but because of who you belong to.

You were handcrafted by the Creator of the universe, and He doesn't make extras or mistakes.

When you doubt your worth, remember this: Sparrows don't hustle for validation. They don't question if they're flying right. They just *do what they were made to do*.

And so should you.

The worth of His plan isn't found in how perfectly you perform it—it's in how faithfully you walk it out.

So, go ahead. Take the step. Speak the truth. Write the book. Love the people.

You are not too broken, too late, or too small for the plan He's written for you.

You are *worthy of it*. Because He said so.

Prayer:

Lord, thank You for trusting me with a purpose that's bigger than my confidence. When I doubt my worth, remind me that You never did. Help me walk boldly in the plan You've chosen for me—not because I'm perfect, but because I'm Yours. Amen.

DAY 60

The Promise in the Plan

> "Those He called, He also justified; those He justified, He also glorified." — *Romans 8:30*

Y'all, I love me some HGTV. When I can't find anything else to watch, it's my go-to—well, that and a good baking championship show. (Something about people stressing over fondant just soothes my soul.)

But I think what really pulls me in is the *transformation*. I love a good before-and-after. There's something so satisfying about watching, in under an hour (okay, 48 minutes if I fast-forward through the commercials) something go from chaos to breathtaking. From broken-down to built-up. From old and ordinary to beautifully new.

If you've ever watched one of those home renovation shows, you know the moment everyone waits for—the *final reveal*.

The cameras roll, the music swells, and the homeowner walks through the front door with tears in their eyes, finally seeing what's been happening behind the scenes.

That's how God's promises work.

For so long, it can feel like all you're surrounded by is sawdust and scaffolding—prayers in process, lessons that don't make sense, walls that got torn down before you could see why. You look around and think, *"What even is this season?"*

But then one day—usually when you least expect it—He lets you step back. And suddenly, it all clicks.

Every delay. Every detour. Every no that made you cry and every closed door that made you question your worth.

It was all part of His design.

You see, God doesn't just hand us blueprints for our lives and wish us luck. He builds with us, step by step, promise by promise.

And when His Word says, "Those He called, He also justified," that's His way of saying, *"I didn't just call you—I equipped you. I made you ready for this."*

The plan was never just about *where* He was leading you—it was about *who* He was shaping you into along the way.

Because God's plans don't just build destinations; they build character.

They teach patience, trust, surrender, and faith that can stand when the storms hit.

And then one day, when the dust settles and you look back at all He's done, you'll see it—His fingerprints on every wall, His promise woven into every detail, His glory reflected in every corner of your story.

The reveal won't just be beautiful—it'll be sacred.

And you'll realize what He's been saying all along:

"I never left you in the mess—I was building the masterpiece."

So if you're still standing in the middle of the construction zone right now, keep trusting.

You're not lost. You're mid-renovation.

And the promise? It's already written into the plan.

Prayer:

Lord, thank You that Your plans never end in confusion, only completion. When I can't see the full picture, help me trust that You're still building. Thank You for every season of dust and design—and for the promise that one day, I'll see the masterpiece You've had in mind all along. Amen.

HIS PROMISE

His Promise

We've spent time sitting in His love—learning who we are because of it.

We've wrestled with His plan—trusting that He's got a purpose for our lives even when it doesn't look like what we pictured.

And now, we get to walk into His promise—the *how* of it all.

If you've been with me this far, you might remember the formula I've shared before—the one that breaks down fulfillment into our *who*, our *why*, and our *how*.

I see now that it was never just a formula for life—it was a reflection of His truth.

Because our *how* has always been about trusting His promise.

Now, I'd love to tell you that I have this all figured out—that I never doubt, never wrestle, never question. But let's be honest, y'all ... I'm still walking this out right alongside you.

I know I'm loved. I know He has a plan for my life. But I still have days when that sneaky voice in my head tries to tell me I'm less than—that maybe I've missed it, maybe I'm behind, maybe I'm not quite enough.

And it's in those moments (the messy, human ones) that I have to stop leaning on my fear and start leaning into His promise.

Because here's what I've learned: His plan is already set. He's thought through every detail—the missteps, the setbacks, and the moments we want to throw in the towel. None of it surprises Him. Not one thing.

So when I start to spiral or second-guess, I remind myself:

I don't have to see the full path to trust the One who paved it.

Faith doesn't mean it won't be uncomfortable.

It means we take a deep breath, whisper *"Okay, God, I trust You,"* and step forward anyway.

And even when my knees are shaking, I know this—He's got me.

Not just got me—He's *gone before me.*

The best part? Every promise He's ever made, He's kept.

Every single one.

So as we move into these next 30 days together, we're going to dig into those promises—the ones that anchor our souls when fear starts to rise. The ones that whisper peace when life feels loud.

Because brave doesn't mean fearless. It means we believe His promise more than we believe our doubts.

So take a breath, friend. We've learned about His love. We've leaned into His plan.

Now, it's time to live in the *confidence of His promise.*

He's not just building your story—He's fulfilling it.

DAY 61

Standing on His Word

"My word ... will accomplish what I desire." — Isaiah 55:11

Here's a wild thought: How many times have you trusted someone (and I mean *really* trusted them) only to have them let you down?

Maybe it was a friend who said, "I'll be there, I promise," and wasn't.

Maybe it was a relationship that started with big words and good intentions but fell flat when things got real.

Maybe it's someone in your life right now who keeps saying all the right things but just can't seem to follow through.

And yet, somehow, we still give them another chance.

We extend more trust, more grace, more belief that *this time* will be different.

But when it comes to God—the One who has *never once* broken a promise, the One whose Word literally cannot fail—we hesitate.

We question.

We doubt.

We trust flaky people with more faith than we trust a flawless God.

Let that sink in for a second.

Now, don't get me wrong—people will disappoint us because they're human. (Lord knows I've disappointed plenty myself.) But God? He's not guessing. He's not overcommitted. He's not making empty promises to make us feel better in the moment.

When He speaks, it's settled.

When He promises, it's already in motion.

When He says He'll do it, *He will.*

Isaiah 55:11 says, "My word will not return to me empty."

That means when God sends His Word out, whether it's a promise, a purpose, or a prayer over your life, it's not coming back unfulfilled.

It *will* accomplish what He intended.

Our feelings may fluctuate. Our circumstances may shift. But His Word? It stands firm—unshaken and unstoppable.

So if He said He'll provide ... He will.

If He said He'll heal ... He will.

If He said He'll redeem, restore, rebuild ... *He will.*

And if He said He loves you—you'd better believe *He always will.*

So maybe today, it's time to shift where you're standing.

Not on feelings.

Not on other people's promises.

But on His Word—the only foundation that never cracks under pressure.

Prayer:

Lord, thank You that Your Word never fails. When I'm tempted to doubt or waver, remind me that Your promises are not fragile—they are forever. Help me to stand on what You've said, not on what I see. Amen.

DAY 62

Unshakable Hope

"Let us hold unswervingly to the hope we profess, for He who promised is faithful." — Hebrews 10:23

In business, we love to say, "Hope is not a strategy."

And when it comes to sales plans, budgets, or quarterly goals—sure, that's probably true. You need data, structure, and action to make things happen.

But with God?

Hope *is* the strategy.

Because when life falls apart—when your plan, your timeline, and your strength all fail you—hope is what keeps you hanging on to the One who never does.

There have been moments in my life where hope was the only thing I had left to hold. Seasons where I was hanging on by a single, frayed thread.

When I dropped out of high school—hope whispered, *He still has a future for you.*

When I was single and pregnant—hope reminded me, *You are not alone. He will fill the gaps others can't.*

When I lost my job—hope steadied my heart with, *He will provide again.*

When I went through divorce—hope whispered, *Healing will come, and joy will return.*

When my dad passed—hope gave me peace that I will see him again in heaven.

And now, even as God calls me into new seasons—seeds of ministry, unknown paths, uncharted territory—hope keeps me moving forward. Because if He's written the plan, I can trust it's a good one.

Hope doesn't mean pretending everything's fine. It means believing that *even when it's not*, God is still faithful.

It's not wishful thinking, it's confident expectation rooted in His character.

Because He's never failed before, and He's not about to start now.

So, when your heart feels heavy and your faith feels thin, hold on.

Grip that hope like it's the lifeline it is.

Because you're not holding onto a theory—you're holding onto *Him*.

And He is faithful. Always.

Prayer:
Lord, thank You for being the anchor of my hope. When life feels uncertain, remind me that my confidence isn't in circumstances, it's in You. Strengthen my faith, steady my heart, and help me to hold unswervingly to the hope I have in You. Amen.

DAY 63

The Peace Promise

"Peace I leave with you; my peace I give you." — *John 14:27*

Let's be honest, peace can feel pretty hard to come by these days. Between the noise of the world, the endless to-do lists, the chasing, the striving, and the comparing—sometimes peace feels like something reserved for monks in the mountains, not women balancing meetings, meals, and a million expectations.

A few years ago, I was invited to speak at the International Builders Show's inaugural prayer breakfast about what women in our industry needed prayer for most.

At first, I was honored. Then I panicked.

I thought, *What in the world am I supposed to say on behalf of thousands of women?*

So I started asking around—calling friends, mentors, and leaders from across the country—and one by one, their answers came in.

But what I received weren't just prayer requests.

They were pieces of broken hearts.

And the more I read, the heavier it felt. I remember praying, "God, what am I supposed to do with all of this?"

And right there—in the stillness of that moment—He met me.

Everything around me got quiet.

And in that sacred hush, I felt Him speak.

I said, "God, they've asked me to pray for a voice."

And He said, *"Amy, I hear their voice. I am listening."*

I said, "They've asked for a seat at the table."

And He said, *"I've already prepared a seat for them at Mine."*

When I brought up equality, He reminded me of His Word—that man is not independent from woman, and woman is not independent from man—because both came from Him.

And when I prayed about opportunity and advancement, He whispered Jeremiah 29:11 straight into my heart: *"For I know the plans I have for you ..."*

It was in that moment I realized what that unfamiliar stillness was.

It was peace.

Not relief. Not success. Not answers.

But peace, the kind that doesn't make sense, the kind that stills your heart even when the world around you feels loud and heavy.

Jesus said, "My peace I give to you." And that's exactly what He offers—not temporary calm or surface-level quiet, but *His* peace. The kind that hushes fear, silences striving, and steadies your soul even in the storm.

That day I told the women in that room what I'll tell you now:

We need peace—peace from imposter syndrome and pressure, peace from the demands of perfection, peace from resentment and comparison.

Because peace doesn't mean everything around you is calm.

It means *Christ* is.

When He's at the center, even the chaos can't shake you.

Prayer:
Lord, thank You for the peace that doesn't make sense but somehow makes everything still. Teach me to rest in Your presence instead of chasing control. Quiet the noise of my world so I can hear Your whisper and feel Your peace today. Amen.

DAY 64

Provision in Every Season

"My God will supply all your needs according to His riches in glory." — Philippians 4:19

There have been so many seasons in my life where I've sat and asked, *"What now, God?"*

You know the ones—when the plan falls apart, the account runs low, the relationship ends, or the opportunity you were counting on suddenly disappears.

Those "How am I going to make it through this?" moments that leave you staring at the ceiling, whispering prayers that sound more like panic.

I've been there—more than once.

When I lost a job and wondered how I'd provide for my family.

When I was a single parent trying to figure out how to make ends meet.

When I had to start over after a failed marriage, piecing my life back together while pretending I was fine.

Every single time, God showed up.

Not always how I expected, not always how I *wanted*, but always *right on time*.

Sometimes His provision came through a job I didn't see coming.

Sometimes through the kindness of a friend, the right conversation, or a door that opened just as another one slammed shut.

And sometimes, His provision wasn't something I could see at all—it was peace when I should've been falling apart. Strength when I had nothing left. A quiet assurance that said, *"I've got you."*

The truth is, God's provision isn't limited to finances or things. It's everything your soul and situation need—grace, guidance, wisdom, peace, patience, people, purpose.

He provides not because we've earned it, but because He's good.

His supply isn't tied to your performance—it's tied to His care.

Philippians 4:19 doesn't say, *"My God might supply …"*

It says, *"My God will."*

And if He's done it before—He'll do it again.

So whatever season you're in right now—whether you're waiting on the next paycheck, the next opportunity, or just the next ounce of strength to keep going—take heart.

He already knows what you need.

And He's already made a way for it.

You might not see it yet, but it's on its way.

> ## *Prayer:*
> *Lord, thank You for being my Provider in every season—the seen and the unseen, the expected and the surprising. When I'm tempted to worry, remind me of all the ways You've shown up before. Teach me to trust Your timing and Your heart more than my circumstances. Amen.*

DAY 65

Never Alone

"The Lord Himself goes before you and will be with you." — *Deuteronomy 31:8*

Loneliness has a way of sneaking up on us, doesn't it?

Sometimes it's loud, like when the house goes quiet after everyone's gone, or when a relationship ends and the silence feels like it echoes.

Other times it's subtle like sitting in a crowded room and still feeling unseen, or smiling your way through the day while your heart quietly whispers, *"Does anyone even notice me?"*

I've had those seasons ... the ones that feel a little empty, a little quieter than usual. When the texts stop coming, the plans slow down, and suddenly it's just you, your thoughts, and a lot of question marks.

But here's the thing I've learned (and keep learning, because apparently, I'm a slow learner in this department): Being alone and *feeling* alone are not the same thing.

Because even in the loneliest seasons—the single-mom years, the starting-over years, the "God, where are You?" years—I was never actually by myself.

He was there.

He was there in the quiet moments when I couldn't see what was next.

He was there in the parking lot tears when I just needed to let it all out.

He was there in the middle of sleepless nights when the what-ifs wouldn't stop spinning.

And every time, when I finally got still enough to listen, I could feel His whisper reminding me:

"*You are not forgotten. You are not abandoned. I am right here.*"

The Lord Himself—not an angel, not a stand-in, not a substitute—*He Himself* goes before you and stays beside you.

That means before you even walk into the next season, He's already been there.

He's already worked out the details you're worrying about.

And He's staying with you through every single step.

That's not just comfort—that's identity.

Because His presence is proof of your worth. He stays because you matter.

So if you're walking through a season that feels a little quiet, remember this:

You might feel unseen, but you are never alone.

Prayer:

Lord, thank You for walking with me through every season— the loud ones, the lonely ones, and the in-between. When I start to feel forgotten, remind me that You are right beside me. Teach me to rest in Your presence, even when I can't see the path ahead. Amen.

DAY 66

Beauty from Ashes

"To bestow on them a crown of beauty
instead of ashes." — *Isaiah 61:3*

Let's talk about ashes.

Because if you've lived long enough, you've probably got a few—the burned-up leftovers of something you thought would last forever. Maybe it was a dream, a relationship, a plan, or just the version of your life you *thought* you'd be living by now.

I've had my fair share of "Well, that went up in flames" seasons.

The ones where I looked around and thought, *"Okay God, this cannot possibly be the plan. Surely, this is a detour, right?"*

(Plot twist: it wasn't a detour. It was the setup.)

There were times when I thought, *"Well, this must be it—this is as good as it gets."*

And if we're being honest, those moments usually found me sitting in sweatpants, eating my feelings, and wondering if Amazon sells purpose on Prime.

But God, in His infinite goodness (and sense of humor), didn't leave me there.

He took the ashes of what I thought was *the end* and started building something new.

And here's what I've learned:

God doesn't just clean up your mess—He *transforms* it.

He doesn't sweep up the ashes and throw them out.

He takes them, reshapes them, and somehow turns them into something beautiful.

Something stronger.

Something that carries more meaning than it ever did before it broke.

When I look back at some of those "ash" seasons—the heartbreak, the job loss, the loneliness, the starting over—I can see His fingerprints all over them. Those were the places where He grew me, refined me, and set me up for things I couldn't have imagined back then.

If I could go back and tell the old me anything, I'd say:

"Girl, don't quit in the ashes—that's where the artist does His best work."

Because now, through His promise, I don't just see possibility—I feel *limitless*.

Not because I've got it all figured out, but because I know the One who does.

The same God who brings beauty from ashes is still writing your story—and trust me, the best chapters haven't even been revealed yet.

Prayer:

Lord, thank You for taking the ashes of my past and turning them into something beautiful. When I'm standing in the smoke, remind me that You're not done—You're just getting started. Teach me to trust Your process, even when I can't see the masterpiece You're creating. Amen.

DAY 66

Beauty from Ashes

"To bestow on them a crown of beauty
instead of ashes." — *Isaiah 61:3*

Let's talk about ashes.

Because if you've lived long enough, you've probably got a few—the burned-up leftovers of something you thought would last forever. Maybe it was a dream, a relationship, a plan, or just the version of your life you *thought* you'd be living by now.

I've had my fair share of "Well, that went up in flames" seasons.

The ones where I looked around and thought, *"Okay God, this cannot possibly be the plan. Surely, this is a detour, right?"*

(Plot twist: it wasn't a detour. It was the setup.)

There were times when I thought, *"Well, this must be it—this is as good as it gets."*

And if we're being honest, those moments usually found me sitting in sweatpants, eating my feelings, and wondering if Amazon sells purpose on Prime.

But God, in His infinite goodness (and sense of humor), didn't leave me there.

He took the ashes of what I thought was *the end* and started building something new.

And here's what I've learned:

God doesn't just clean up your mess—He *transforms* it.

He doesn't sweep up the ashes and throw them out.

He takes them, reshapes them, and somehow turns them into something beautiful.

Something stronger.

Something that carries more meaning than it ever did before it broke.

When I look back at some of those "ash" seasons—the heartbreak, the job loss, the loneliness, the starting over—I can see His fingerprints all over them. Those were the places where He grew me, refined me, and set me up for things I couldn't have imagined back then.

If I could go back and tell the old me anything, I'd say:

"Girl, don't quit in the ashes—that's where the artist does His best work."

Because now, through His promise, I don't just see possibility—I feel *limitless*.

Not because I've got it all figured out, but because I know the One who does.

The same God who brings beauty from ashes is still writing your story—and trust me, the best chapters haven't even been revealed yet.

Prayer:
Lord, thank You for taking the ashes of my past and turning them into something beautiful. When I'm standing in the smoke, remind me that You're not done—You're just getting started. Teach me to trust Your process, even when I can't see the masterpiece You're creating. Amen.

DAY 67

Strength Renewed

"Those who hope in the Lord will renew their strength." — *Isaiah 40:31*

If you've ever been in a season where you're running on fumes, caffeine, and the occasional burst of adrenaline that feels suspiciously like anxiety ... same.

Lately, I've been living in this weird rhythm where my mental soundtrack goes something like:

8 a.m.—*I'm ok.*

12 p.m. —*Am I ok?*

2 p.m. —*Nope. Definitely not ok!*

Repeat daily.

It's the season of doing "all the things"—the work, the family, the callings, the expectations—while still trying to be the version of myself who drinks enough water and prays without falling asleep. Some days, I feel like I'm absolutely crushing it. Other days, it feels more like the crushing is happening *to me*.

Can you relate?

Here's the truth: I'm not burned out—I'm *poured out*. There's a difference.

And yet even when I'm emptied, God keeps refilling.

Because here's the promise: *Those who hope in the Lord will renew their strength.*

Not "might." Not "if you get enough sleep."

They **will**.

That means when I'm tired, He's not.

When I'm unsure, He's steady.

When I feel less than, He's reminding me that through His strength, I'm more than capable.

I've learned that "renewal" doesn't always mean rest—sometimes it means *reliance*.

It's not about trying harder; it's about leaning harder.

And if we're honest, some of us (me included) have to get to the point of total exhaustion before we finally stop trying to do it all on our own and say,

"Okay, God ... You drive. I'm just going to take a nap in the passenger seat."

So if you're in a season where the grind is real and your "I'm fine" face is starting to twitch—take heart. You're not failing; you're just being reminded to refuel.

Your tank might be empty, but His supply never is.

Prayer:

Lord, when I'm running on empty, remind me that You're my source—not my schedule, not my success, not my strength. Renew me from the inside out and teach me to lean on Your power, not my own performance. Amen.

DAY 68

The Promise Keeper

"For no matter how many promises God has made, they are 'Yes' in Christ." — 2 Corinthians 1:20

You know how some people are just *not* great at keeping promises?

Like, "I promise I'll call you back," or "I promise I'll only have one glass of wine," or my personal favorite—"I promise this meeting won't take long."

(We've all been lied to.)

The truth is, humans are flaky. We mean well, but we get distracted, forgetful, or flat-out tired.

And if we're honest, sometimes we start projecting that same unreliable pattern onto God—like maybe *His* promise is subject to delays, fine print, or terms and conditions we didn't read.

But they're not.

God doesn't deal in "maybes."

He doesn't make half-commitments or empty reassurances.

Every single one of His promises—from peace and provision to purpose and redemption—is a firm, heaven-stamped YES in Christ.

That means when life looks uncertain, His word isn't.

When people flake, He stays faithful.

And when we're doubting whether things are still on track, Jesus Himself is the guarantee that the answer is *still yes*.

I don't know about you, but I've needed that reminder lately.

Because there are days I wake up with more questions than

confidence, and I catch myself asking, "But what if this isn't going to work out? What if I missed it?"

And then I remember, God doesn't ghost His people.

He keeps His word. Every. Single. Time.

His promise isn't based on my performance; it's sealed by His perfection.

So instead of living in doubt or delay, I can rest in His *Yes*—and my *Amen*.

That's where peace lives.

That's where confidence grows.

That's where the shaky "I hope so" faith turns into "I know so" assurance.

So, whatever you're waiting on today, remember this:

If He said it, He'll do it.

He's not just the maker of promises—He's the keeper of them.

Prayer:

Lord, thank You for being faithful to every promise You've ever made. When I start to doubt Your timing, remind me of Your track record. Help me live with "Yes and Amen" confidence—resting not in what I see, but in what You've already said. Amen.

DAY 69

The Gift of Grace

"For it is by grace you have been saved,
through faith." — *Ephesians 2:8*

Let's get one thing straight, grace is not a performance review.

I spent *years* trying to earn what God had already given me.

I treated grace like it was some sort of rewards program—the "Holy Gold Membership" where if I did enough good things, prayed enough fancy prayers, and didn't lose my temper in traffic, I could earn a few extra points toward blessing.

Spoiler alert: That's not how grace works.

Grace is not a paycheck you earn; it's a gift you receive.

And not because you nailed it.

Because *He did*.

It took me a long time to understand that I don't have to hustle for holy approval.

I don't have to prove my worth to the One who already decided I was worth dying for.

My striving doesn't strengthen His love—it just exhausts me trying to earn something that's already mine.

If you're anything like me, you might still fall into that trap sometimes—striving to be the best, to get it all right, to feel *enough*.

But grace gently whispers,

"Stop trying so hard. You already are."

Because your worth was settled at the cross.

Grace signed the paperwork.

Jesus stamped it "paid in full."

It's not a prize for the perfect—it's a promise for the imperfect.

And praise God for that, because if perfection was the requirement, I'd be disqualified before breakfast most days.

So today, instead of striving, rest.

Instead of earning, receive.

Instead of doubting your value, remember that it was already proven, once and for all, by the greatest act of love in history.

You don't have to work your way to grace.

You just have to walk in it.

Prayer:
Lord, thank You for the gift of grace—unearned, undeserved, but freely given. Help me stop striving for what You've already settled. Let me rest in the truth that I am loved, chosen, and covered by Your grace today and every day. Amen.

DAY 70

Faith Over Fear

"Be strong and courageous. Do not be afraid ... for the Lord your God will be with you." — *Joshua 1:9*

You've probably heard me call myself a "Brave Expert."

Sounds pretty *bad a-double-s*, right? (hey, it doesn't count if you spell it instead of say it, where's my Christian cussys at?)

Truth is, I'm not a brave expert because I've mastered courage—I'm a brave expert because I've spent a *lot* of time being afraid.

Fear of not being enough.

Fear of being too much.

Fear of failing, missing it, or worse—finding out I actually *could've* done it, but didn't.

Yeah, I've been a frequent flyer in the fear zone.

For years, I thought bravery meant pushing through it—showing up strong, smiling wide, and pretending I wasn't terrified.

But here's what I've learned:

Being brave isn't about eliminating fear.

It's about *choosing faith in the middle of it.*

And it turns out, courage has never really been about *my* ability—it's always been about *His*.

When I look back, I can see how even my shaky, half-hearted steps were guided. Every stumble, every detour, every moment I thought I'd fallen too far off course—He was still there, redirecting, redeeming, rerouting.

Faith doesn't cancel fear; it just refuses to let fear drive.

And every time I've chosen faith (even the trembling kind) I've seen His promise unfold in ways that my fear could never have planned.

So if you're reading this and you feel stuck between faith and fear—congratulations. That's the perfect place for a miracle.

Because courage isn't about never being scared; it's about trusting Who walks with you through it.

You don't have to have it all figured out.

You just have to take the next brave step—knowing you're not taking it alone.

Prayer:
Lord, thank You for being with me in every moment—the bold and the trembling. When fear tries to steal my focus, remind me that faith isn't about my strength but Yours. Help me walk boldly, trusting that every step is guided by Your hand. Amen.

DAY 71

Joy Comes in the Morning

> "Weeping may stay for the night, but joy comes in the morning." — *Psalm 30:5*

There's a sacred kind of ache that comes with loss.

The kind that changes you, softens you, and makes you see life a little differently.

I've lived through a few seasons of loss—some replaceable, like jobs or opportunities that slipped through my fingers, and others that left a permanent mark, like losing my dad ten years ago.

He was my best friend, my biggest cheerleader, and one of the best humans I've ever known.

Even after a decade, the sting still lingers. Grief is funny that way, it never fully goes away; it just changes its shape. But here's what I've learned: God doesn't leave us in the dark forever.

The nights of sorrow—they have an expiration date.

And when morning comes, joy comes with it.

That doesn't mean joy replaces the grief or that we suddenly stop missing what was lost. It means that His presence meets us right there in the middle of it.

He walks with us through the dark valleys, sits beside us when we can barely speak and our faces are swollen from all the tears cried, and gently reminds us that this isn't the end of the story.

For me, the joy looks like this: knowing my dad has been made new, that I'll see him again one day, and that every tear shed in this life will be wiped away in the next.

That's the promise of His presence—He walks with us in the sorrow *and* in the sunrise.

And maybe your "night" looks different.

Maybe it's the loss of a relationship, a dream, or a version of your life that no longer exists.

Whatever it is, hold tight, because joy *will* come. It might tip-toe in quietly instead of bursting through the door, but it's coming.

You won't cry forever.

You won't hurt forever.

And you're never walking through any of it alone.

Because the same God who promises joy in the morning is the One who holds you through the night.

Prayer:
Lord, thank You for walking with me through every season—through loss, through waiting, through the nights that feel endless. Remind me that even in sorrow, You are near and joy is on its way. Thank You for the promise of reunion, renewal, and unending joy in You. Amen.

DAY 72

Guarded by Peace

"The peace of God ... will guard your hearts and minds in Christ Jesus." — *Philippians 4:7*

You ever wish you had a full-time bodyguard?

Someone to step between you and whatever is trying to ruin your peace—the email that hits wrong, the group text that spirals, the self-doubt that sneaks in at 2 a.m.?

Same.

But here's the good news—you *do* have one. His name is Peace.

God's peace isn't just a gentle breeze or a spa-day feeling (though, Lord knows, I'll never turn either down).

His peace is a *guard*—a divine security system standing watch over your heart and mind.

It's what keeps the chaos from breaking in and stealing your joy.

I've had seasons where I needed that guard more than ever.

Moments when my thoughts ran wild—what-ifs, worst-case scenarios, the "What am I even doing with my life" loop playing on repeat.

But every time I came back to Him, His peace showed up like a bouncer at the door, saying, "Sorry, fear—you're not on the list tonight."

And here's what I've realized: Peace is proof of trust.

When you believe you're loved, protected, and chosen—when

you understand your infinite worth in Christ—anxiety loses its leverage.

You don't have to fight every battle that knocks; some things are better left to your divine security detail.

So if life feels noisy right now, take a deep breath.

Let His peace do what it's designed to do—*guard you.*

You don't have to white-knuckle control or explain your calm.

You can simply rest, knowing the One who holds your heart never sleeps on duty.

> *Prayer:*
> *Lord, thank You for the peace that doesn't just comfort me but guards me. When my thoughts spiral and my heart feels heavy, remind me that Your presence is my protection. Let Your peace stand watch over my mind and keep my heart steady in You. Amen.*

DAY 73

Firm Foundation

"The wise man built his house on the rock." — *Matthew 7:24–25*

If there's one thing my career in homebuilding has taught me, it's this: A house is only as strong as what it's standing on.

You can have the most stunning design, the dream kitchen, the fancy finishes—but if the foundation isn't solid, one good storm will tell the truth.

And let me tell you, life comes with plenty of storms.

As a homebuilder, I've walked through new communities before the first wall ever went up—nothing but dirt, blueprints, and faith in what *will be*.

It's funny how similar that feels to life sometimes. You can have the vision, the plan, even the materials, but without the right foundation—one anchored in something (or Someone) unshakable—it all starts to crack under pressure.

I've built a few of my own "homes" on sandy ground before.

There were seasons when I built my worth on approval, my confidence on achievement, and my peace on things that could change overnight.

And when the storm came—whether it was loss, failure, rejection, or just a good old-fashioned identity crisis—it all started to crumble.

But God, in His mercy, let a few of those houses fall so I could finally rebuild on something real.

Because His promise? It doesn't shift.

It doesn't settle.

It holds.

The truth is, the wise builder doesn't avoid storms—she just prepares for them.

She digs deep, sets her footing on faith, and knows that no matter how hard the wind blows, she's not going down.

So if you feel like everything around you is shaking, don't panic—it might just be God testing the soil beneath your feet.

He's not punishing you; He's fortifying you.

He's making sure what's being built next can actually stand.

And friend, it will. Because when you build your life on His Word, you're not just building a house—you're building a home that lasts.

Prayer:
Lord, thank You for being my firm foundation when life feels unsteady. Teach me to build on Your promises, not my emotions. When the storms come, remind me that I'm not just standing with You—I'm standing on You. Amen.

DAY 74

Redeemed and Restored

"I will restore to you the years that the
locusts have eaten." — *Joel 2:25*

If there's one thing I've learned about God, it's that He doesn't do waste. Not with time, not with pain, not with people.

There are years of my life I wish I could get back. Seasons that felt like detours or full-blown disasters. Years when I made choices out of fear instead of faith. Moments I look back on and think, "If I'd just done this differently … "

But here's the truth that sets my heart at peace every single time: God doesn't need a do-over to bring restoration. He can redeem right from where you are.

Maybe you've had seasons where everything felt stripped away—relationships, opportunities, joy, even hope. The locusts in your life came and did their thing, and you've been left staring at what feels like ruins. I get that.

But this verse, this promise, reminds us that God is the ultimate restorer. He doesn't just patch things up. He rebuilds them better.

The enemy's favorite lie is that it's too late. That you've missed your moment, wasted your best years, or ruined your shot. But God's not looking at your past shaking His head—He's already working on your comeback story.

When I look back at the parts of my life that felt lost or broken, I can see His fingerprints all over the restoration. He brought beauty out of the pieces, purpose out of the pain, and peace out of the chaos.

Nothing wasted. Nothing beyond redemption.

If He can redeem years, He can redeem anything. Your mistakes, your heartbreak, your time, your dreams—all of it.

You are not too far gone, and nothing you've lost is too far out of His reach.

Redemption isn't just something He does. It's who He is.

> *Prayer:*
> *Lord, thank You for being the God of restoration. For every year, every dream, every part of me that felt lost, I trust that You are redeeming it for something good. Help me to release regret and walk confidently into the story You're still writing. Amen.*

DAY 75

His Promise: Redeemed Confidence

"Those who look to him are radiant; their faces are never covered with shame" — *Psalm 34:5*

Some mornings, the mirror is not giving "beloved daughter of the King."

It's giving:

pillow-creased face,

eyes that look like they've seen some things, and

a rogue chin hair that clearly didn't ask permission.

And just like that, the self-criticism starts.

When I start treating my reflection like a courtroom, I think of a woman in the Bible with unshakeable faith. You can find her story in *Mark 5:25–34* and *Luke 8:43–48*.

Scripture tells us she had been bleeding for twelve years. Twelve years.

And in that culture, that meant more than physical suffering—it meant isolation. She would have been considered unclean, pushed to the margins, unable to fully participate in community, worship, or ordinary life. If anyone had reason to believe she was "less than," it was her.

Yet, she did something extraordinary:

She pushed through the crowd—through the shame, the stares, the barriers—and reached for Jesus' cloak, believing:

"If I can just touch Him, I will be healed."
And Jesus didn't turn away from her condition.
He turned toward her identity.
He called her Daughter.
Not "unclean."
Not "the woman with issues."
Daughter—seen, loved, and restored.
And if Jesus spoke *that* over her, He speaks it over you, too.

Because here's the truth we forget when we're side-eyeing ourselves in the mirror:

God's promises don't just redeem your past—they redeem your perception.

He promised beauty instead of ashes.

He promised a crown instead of shame.

He promised belovedness instead of comparison.

You are not a before-picture waiting for an after.

You are a masterpiece in motion—and the Artist doesn't regret His work.

So maybe tomorrow morning, when the lighting is rude and your inner critic tries to clock in early, pause and say:

"Lord, help me see what You see."

Because confidence isn't pretending you love every detail—it's trusting the One who designed every detail.

This isn't about vanity.

It's about value.

And sister, your value was settled long before you ever stood in front of a mirror.

Prayer:

Lord, thank You for the promise of beauty from ashes. When I am tempted to see myself through the lens of insecurity or comparison, remind me that You call me Daughter. Teach me to trust what You say about me more than what I feel about me. Redeem my vision of myself until I see Your masterpiece looking back. In Jesus' name, Amen

DAY 76

Light in the Darkness

"I am the light of the world." — *John 8:12*

2015.

Whew. Just saying that year out loud still makes my shoulders tighten a bit. It was one of the hardest years of my life—a blur of blessings, heartbreaks, and spiritual warfare all tangled together.

I had just been promoted to sales manager—which was a huge opportunity and, considering I had *zero* sales experience, a total "God, You sure about this?" moment. The ink was barely dry on the announcement before life started to unravel.

My dad—my best friend, my biggest fan—went in for what was supposed to be a simple outpatient surgery. Instead, complications turned it into almost two months in the hospital. Infection. Pain. Waiting. My mom cared for him endlessly, and when she finally took a much-needed break, I stepped in.

For 21 days, I balanced caring for him with my new role at work, raising small kids, helping with homework, cooking dinner, and holding it all together with a prayer and a to-do list.

Just when I thought I might be catching my breath, my grandfather—my mom's dad, one of the kindest souls I've ever known—passed away.

Not long after, my marriage fell apart.

And then, the unimaginable.

My dad, the one who had been my anchor, my steady place, my person, passed away after complications from a second surgery.

It felt like every light in my life had gone out at once.

If life were a movie, I would've gladly hit the fast-forward button through that year. It was dark—heartbreak after heartbreak, loss after loss. And yet ... even in the middle of all that pain, God was there.

Looking back, I can see Him in the tiniest details—in the people who showed up when I couldn't stand on my own, in the unexpected peace that somehow found me in the hospital room, in the quiet moments when I felt completely alone but wasn't.

I didn't see a floodlight that year—just a flicker.

But that flicker was enough.

Because His promise was never that we'd see the whole road, just that His light would guide us one step at a time.

If you're walking through your own dark season right now, I get it. You're not broken for feeling that way.

But hear me—darkness doesn't mean God's absent. Sometimes, it's just the backdrop that makes His light shine brighter.

So take the next step, even if it's shaky. He's already lighting the way.

Prayer:

Lord, thank You for being my light when everything around me feels dark. When I can't see what's ahead, help me trust that You're already there. Remind me that even one small flicker of Your presence is enough to guide me forward. Amen.

DAY 77

Eternal Perspective

> "Our light and momentary troubles are achieving for us an eternal glory that far outweighs them all." — *2 Corinthians 4:17–18*

I don't know about you, but sometimes I read verses like this and think, "Light and momentary? Really, Paul? Have you *seen* my inbox?"

Let's be real—most of what stresses us out today won't even matter next week, let alone in eternity. But somehow, we let the Wi-Fi going down, the group text drama, or that email that starts with "per my last message" derail our entire mood.

Guilty as charged.

This verse is such a good reminder that this world—with all its noise, chaos, and caffeine dependency—isn't the end of the story. Every hard thing we walk through, every trial we endure, every messy middle moment is shaping something eternal in us.

And listen, I know "eternal perspective" sounds deep and holy, but sometimes it's as simple as asking, "Will this matter in five years?" or even, "Will this matter by Friday?" Most of the time, the answer is no.

That's not to say our pain isn't real—it is. But it's also temporary. The bad day ends. The hard season shifts. The heartbreak heals.

I once heard someone say that if you're looking at life through the lens of eternity, even your worst days are just a bad five minutes on the timeline of forever. And that perspective changes everything.

Because the truth is, you're not working toward some temporary validation—the promotion, the likes, the approval. You're working toward eternal glory. You're investing in something that can't be taken, canceled, or outdone.

So next time you find yourself spinning out over something small (like the fact that someone ate your leftovers), take a breath. Zoom out.

Remember: This world is just the warm-up. The main event is still to come.

> *Prayer:*
> *Lord, thank You for reminding me that my story doesn't end here. Help me keep eternity in focus when temporary troubles try to take over my thoughts. Teach me to laugh, to loosen my grip, and to live for what lasts forever. Amen.*

DAY 78

He Fights for You

"The Lord will fight for you; you need only to be still." — *Exodus 14:14*

Confession time: I'm a bit of a control freak.

There, I said it.

I like things done a certain way, and that certain way is usually *my* way.

My inner dialogue sounds something like: "If I want it done right, I'll do it myself." (Which, in theory, sounds efficient—until you realize you've also appointed yourself CEO of Every Battle That Was Never Yours To Begin With.)

That verse about "being still"? Yeah, I struggle with that one. Because when things get messy, my first instinct isn't to sit quietly and trust God. It's to grab a metaphorical mop, start cleaning, strategizing, fixing, and controlling.

But here's the problem: Every time I try to handle it all in my own strength, I lose peace faster than I can say, "It's fine, I've got it." Spoiler alert—I never "got it."

What I've learned, and let's be honest, still have to relearn about every three days—is that no one fights for me like God does. No one sees the full battlefield like He does. And no one, not even this Type A overachiever, can out-strategize the Creator of the universe.

So why do I cling so tightly to things He's already said He'd handle?

It's the human in me—the part that wants to control what I can see instead of trusting what I can't. But that's where faith kicks in.

Surrender isn't weakness; it's wisdom.

Sometimes the bravest thing you can do isn't to fight harder—it's to stop swinging and let Him fight for you. Because He's not just good at it—He's actually undefeated.

So, if you're weary from trying to fix everything and everyone, take a deep breath. Loosen your grip. You don't have to control what's already covered.

He's fighting for you—and He's never lost a battle yet.

> *Prayer:*
> *Lord, thank You for being my defender when I get tired of defending myself. Help me to trust You enough to let go—to stop striving and start resting in the truth that You're already fighting for me. Amen.*

DAY 79

Chosen and Kept

"To Him who is able to keep you from stumbling." — *Jude 1:24*

Let's just go ahead and get this out of the way—I am, without question, the most imperfect perfectionist you will ever meet.

If there were an Olympic sport for stumbling through temptation, overthinking, or saying "I'm fine" while clearly not being fine, I'd be walking away with the gold medal—possibly two.

I am what I like to call a "hot mess with high standards." My intentions are great. My execution? Questionable at best.

Can anyone else relate?

I mean, I love Jesus—deeply. But I also love snacks after 9 p.m., scrolling when I should be praying, saying things I immediately wish I could stuff back into my mouth like leftover birthday cake, and I've been known to be a little inappropriate at times—hilarious, but inappropriate.

Temptation comes in all kinds of packages, doesn't it?

And somehow, in my messy, distracted, emotional, occasionally inappropriate humanness, God keeps me.

That's what I love about this verse. It's not about my ability to hold on to Him—it's about His promise to hold on to *me*.

Because if it were up to my self-control or my schedule or my spiritual consistency ... well, let's just say we'd all be in trouble.

But He keeps me. He sustains me. He catches me before I

faceplant into whatever mess I've managed to create this week—and when I do trip (which, let's be honest, happens often), He doesn't roll His eyes or say, "Really, Amy?"

He reaches down, picks me up, and says, "Still chosen. Still mine."

So if you've been feeling like you're one mistake away from losing His favor—stop right there. You're not barely hanging on. You're being held. Firmly. Faithfully. Forever.

And that, my friend, is the most freeing thing in the world for an imperfect perfectionist like me.

> *Prayer:*
> *Lord, thank You for loving me through my messy middle moments. When I stumble, remind me that You're not keeping score—You're keeping me. Help me rest in Your steady grip and remember that being chosen means being kept. Amen.*

DAY 80

The Crown of Life

"Blessed is the one who perseveres under trial ... they will receive the crown of life." — James 1:12

If you've made it this far in the devotional, you already know—I'm a bit of a beautiful mess.

I've talked a lot about my humanness, my flaws, my control issues, and my uncanny ability to trip over my own spiritual shoelaces.

But here's the thing: Knowing that God meets me right where I am doesn't mean I get a free pass to just stay there. His grace isn't an excuse for bad behavior—it's an invitation to transformation.

Because being loved unconditionally doesn't mean living irresponsibly.

And I'll be the first to admit, faithfulness isn't always glamorous. It's not mountaintop moments and hallelujah hands every day. Sometimes it looks like showing up when you're tired, praying when you'd rather scroll, forgiving when you'd rather vent, and trusting when you'd rather control.

But that's where the "crown of life" comes in. It's not about perfection—it's about perseverance. It's about staying faithful in the unseen, in the middle of the mundane, when no one's clapping or noticing.

When you choose obedience over ease ...

Forgiveness over frustration ...

Faith over fear ...

That's when you're building something eternal.

God never said this life would be easy—but He did promise it would be worth it. Every act of faithfulness, every surrendered "yes," every time you keep going when quitting would be easier—it's all adding up to something far greater than you can see right now.

So, keep going, messy perfectionist. Keep loving, trusting, stumbling, and standing back up. Because the same God who called you is the one who's cheering you on—crown in hand, waiting to say, "Well done."

Prayer:
Lord, thank You for meeting me in my mess but loving me too much to leave me there. Help me stay faithful in the unseen, steady in the trials, and focused on the eternal reward that's waiting on the other side of obedience. Amen.

DAY 81

The Promise of People

"As iron sharpens iron, so one person sharpens another." — Proverbs 27:17

Adulthood can be a strange season when it comes to friendship. We're juggling careers, families, responsibilities, and our own growth—and finding like-minded women who are in the same stage of life can feel nearly impossible. The truth is, many of us have walked through stretches where we've wondered, *"Where are my people?"*

But God is faithful to His promise of community.

Recently, I spent a few days in Chicago with a group of women who have become like family. We're spread across states, our schedules are full, and months can pass between phone calls—yet if one of us needs the others, we show up *fast*. These aren't surface-level friends; they're the kind who know your dreams, your battles, and your calling. The kind who will pray with you, cry with you, and cheer the loudest when you step into what God's called you to do.

I didn't go searching for them—God sent them. Over time, I've learned that His promise doesn't always come in grand gestures; sometimes it arrives as people.

If you're in a season where friendships feel hard or rare, don't lose hope. God knows how to send the right people—the ones who speak life into your calling, remind you who you are, and love you without keeping score. These relationships are sacred—evidence that His love doesn't just come from heaven, it shows up in the faces around us.

When we find them, we recognize they were never coincidences. They're promises—fulfilled through people.

> *Prayer:*
> *Lord, thank You for the gift of people who make me feel seen and supported. Thank You for friends and family who remind me of Your faithfulness in the way they love, listen, and show up. Help me never take those relationships for granted, and teach me to be that kind of friend for others—steady, loyal, and full of grace. Amen.*

DAY 82

The Promise of Renewal

"Though outwardly we are wasting away, yet inwardly we are being renewed day by day." — 2 Corinthians 4:16

I'll be honest, I've been feeling burned out for months. The joy I used to wake up with, the spark I felt when walking into work, that general zest for life that made me, *me* ... it all started fading.

Now, yes, it's been a tough year in the industry (hello, housing market), but this felt deeper than that. I finally realized—I'm not burnt out. I'm *poured out*.

There's a big difference. Burnout happens when you're running on empty. Poured out happens when you've been giving so much of yourself that there's nothing left to refill—not because you didn't care, but because you didn't pause long enough to let God pour *back in*.

Part of it was the workload—the long days, the endless demands, the constant push to be "on." But another part? It was my resistance to the calling He's been gently whispering for a while now. The one I kept saying, "Not yet, Lord. I'll get to that once I have more time."

But just like in Pure Barre (because of course I'm going to bring a Barre analogy into this), when we pull off the barre, the correct form requires full extension—arms out, trusting the hold. Yet I watch new clients bend their elbows, gripping tighter, making it harder on themselves because they don't trust the form enough to *let go*.

And that's me. That's us. We're gripping our own plans so tight that we're exhausting ourselves trying to hold it all together, when God's saying, "Just extend. Trust Me. Lean into it. I've got you."

Renewal doesn't happen when you have it all together—it happens when you finally stop trying to.

It's not about perfection; it's about permission. Letting Him step into the places you've been white-knuckling and saying, "Lord, I'm tired. Please take it from here."

Because the promise of renewal isn't about making you perfect. It's about making you *new*—over and over again, one surrendered day at a time.

So, if you're feeling poured out, exhausted, or like your joy took an unapproved leave of absence, take heart. You're not broken. You're being rebuilt.

And the One doing the rebuilding? He never runs out of energy, grace, or plans for your life.

> *Prayer:*
> *Lord, thank You for seeing me when I'm tired and meeting me with renewal instead of judgment. Help me let go of what I've been gripping too tightly and trust You to refill what's been poured out. Make me new again today and every day after. Amen.*

DAY 83

Overflow

"My cup overflows." — *Psalm 23:5*

Yesterday I talked about being poured out—that place where you're running on fumes and wondering if maybe caffeine counts as a spiritual gift. (If so, I'm definitely walking in my calling.)

But today? Today I want to talk about *overflow*.

See, being poured out isn't the end of the story. It's the setup for something better—being filled again, this time with what actually sustains you. Because when we stop trying to refill ourselves with more striving, more doing, or more "I've got this," we finally make room for God to pour in His peace, His strength, and His purpose.

And here's the beautiful part: When He fills you, He doesn't stop at "just enough." He keeps pouring until it spills over the rim. That's what His promise does—it overflows.

Overflow doesn't mean excess; it means *sufficiency*. It's that steady, quiet assurance that even when life feels uncertain, *you're still full*. Full of grace, full of purpose, full of love that doesn't depend on your performance.

Because when you live knowing your value in Christ—that you are chosen, loved, and purposed—you stop living from empty. You start living from overflow.

It's not about hustling harder or fixing your own leaks; it's about staying connected to the Source. The more you allow Him to pour into you, the more you naturally pour into others—encouragement, kindness, peace, joy, hope.

And here's what I've learned: When I try to pour from my own cup, I end up exhausted. But when I let God do the pouring, everyone around me gets a taste of His goodness—not my striving.

So if you're feeling empty, don't shame yourself for it. Just bring your cup back to the Source. He's not mad that you ran dry—He's just ready to fill you again.

> ## *Prayer:*
> *Lord, thank You for being the endless Source of all I need. Fill my cup until it overflows with Your peace, joy, and love. And when I pour into others, let it be from Your abundance, not my exhaustion. Amen.*

DAY 84

Unmovable Confidence

"I keep my eyes always on the Lord. With Him at my right hand, I will not be shaken." — Psalm 16:8

We've spent a lot of time together on this journey learning about how deeply loved we are, how intentionally we were created, and how God's promises shape a life of abundance and purpose.

All of those truths speak to the immeasurable value He's placed in you. And hopefully by now, you're starting to not just *know* that—but to *feel* it.

But here's the tricky part ... knowing your worth in Christ and walking in it confidently are two totally different things.

It's one thing to believe in your heart that you're chosen, called, and equipped. It's another to carry that belief into your daily life—to show up in rooms where you feel unqualified, to speak when your voice shakes, to step forward even when your knees do too.

As women, we wrestle with this so much. We can quote affirmations all day long: "I am enough," "I am strong," "I am capable"—but then we catch a glimpse of ourselves in the mirror, remember the one thing that didn't go as planned, or scroll past someone else's highlight reel ... and suddenly, we shrink.

But here's the truth: Confidence isn't arrogance. It's not loud or showy or something you manufacture. It's quiet assurance, the kind that comes from keeping your eyes fixed on *Him*, not on yourself.

When your confidence is rooted in what you can do, it wavers with your performance.

When it's rooted in who He is, it stands unshaken—even when life gets messy.

That's the kind of confidence God wants for you. The kind that doesn't depend on your outfit, your success, your productivity, or your "togetherness." The kind that says, *"Even when I don't feel ready, I know who walks beside me."*

Because confidence built on Him doesn't crumble under pressure—it grows stronger.

So, when that voice in your head starts whispering that you're not enough, remind it that your confidence doesn't come from comparison—it comes from *Christ.*

And He doesn't shake. So neither will you.

Prayer:
Lord, thank You that my confidence isn't found in what I do, but in who You are. When doubt creeps in, remind me that You're at my right hand—steady, strong, and unshakable. Help me walk boldly in the value You've placed in me. Amen.

DAY 85

The Promise of Rest

*"Come to me, all you who are weary and burdened,
and I will give you rest." — Matthew 11:28*

Last year, this verse basically stalked me. I'm not kidding. It was like God was whispering, "Hey ... slow down," but I was too busy trying to keep up to hear Him clearly.

Then one night, I was watching *The Chosen* and it was the episode with the sermon where Jesus said this verse. It hit me so hard that I actually said out loud, "Hmm." Like the kind of *hmm* where you know you've just been spiritually smacked upside the head.

I tried to brush it off, but God wasn't having it. Within days, two friends texted me *that exact same verse*, saying it had been put on their hearts for me. Then it started popping up everywhere—conversations, Pinterest boards, devotionals, random sermon clips on Instagram. I mean, I half-expected it to show up on my Starbucks cup at that point.

And the wild part? I was *exhausted*. Running on empty, striving instead of trusting, busy doing good things but not necessarily *God things*. Somewhere along the way, I'd started moving in the wrong direction with my calling—not in rebellion, just in rhythm with the wrong pace.

So, I finally surrendered. I took what I told myself would be a "30-day season of rest." Just 30 days to breathe, listen, and see what was next ... even though, deep down, I kind of already knew what He was telling me. (And if we're being honest, I also knew I'd resist it. You know, just to be *sure* I was hearing Him right, of course.)

Those 30 days turned into almost three months. Three months of quiet. Three months of conviction. Three months of sitting still when my natural instinct was to sprint.

And when I came back—because I had a speaking commitment and figured it was time to jump back in—something still felt off. That off-ness led to giving a bunch of wrong "yeses" and just going through the motions, which eventually turned into full-on paralysis.

Looking back now, I see what God was doing. The rest wasn't punishment. It was preparation. He was clearing space for clarity, stripping away my need to perform, and teaching me that His kind of rest isn't about pausing your purpose—it's about powering it *through Him*.

Rest isn't laziness. It's trust.

It's saying, "God, You can handle what I'm trying so hard to control."

So if you're weary, stretched too thin, or trying to outrun burnout (or poured out), take it from someone who tried that and lost—the invitation still stands. "Come to Me."

You don't need to earn rest. You just need to receive it.

Prayer:
Lord, thank You for calling me to rest—not because I've earned it, but because I need it. Help me release the constant striving and find peace in Your presence. Quiet my mind, steady my heart, and let me rest in the confidence that You're working even while I'm still. Amen.

DAY 86

The Promise of Freedom

"So if the Son sets you free, you will be free indeed." — *John 8:36*

Freedom. It's one of those words that sounds big and bold—like fireworks and declarations and fresh starts. But if I'm being honest, the kind of freedom Jesus offers doesn't always feel flashy. Sometimes it feels more like exhaling after holding your breath for way too long.

For most of my life, I thought freedom meant finally getting everything under control—my stress, my sin, my schedule, my people-pleasing tendencies. (Spoiler: I'm still waiting for that day.) I thought once I fixed enough of myself, *then* I'd finally feel free.

But here's what I've learned: freedom isn't something we achieve, it's something we *receive*.

When you give your life to Him—your worries, your striving, your guilt, your mess-ups, all of it—you're not just surrendering; you're *unlocking*. Because true freedom isn't about doing whatever you want; it's about finally being free from what's been holding you hostage.

For me, that's looked like releasing shame over the past, forgiving myself for choices I can't redo, and learning (slowly) to stop carrying responsibilities God never asked me to hold. Every time I lay something down—a fear, a failure, a false narrative—I can almost feel the chains loosen.

And you know what's wild? The freedom He gives doesn't depend on my getting it all right. It's already done. The cross settled it. The resurrection sealed it.

So why do we keep living like we're still imprisoned? Why do we walk around dragging our guilt like a designer bag we can't let go of? (Asking for a friend ... and by "friend," I mean me.)

Here's the truth: When Jesus said *you are free indeed*, He didn't add an asterisk. No fine print. No "once you get your act together." Just *free*.

Freedom from shame.

Freedom from striving.

Freedom from trying to earn what's already been given.

So take a deep breath, friend. You don't have to hustle for grace. You don't have to carry what He already nailed to the cross. You are free—completely, totally, and beautifully free.

Now go live like it.

Prayer:
Lord, thank You for the freedom You've already given me—freedom from shame, from fear, and from the need to prove myself. Help me walk in that truth every day, unchained and unburdened, fully trusting that You've already paid it all. Amen.

DAY 87

The Promise of Purpose in Every Season

"In all things God works for the good of those who love Him." — *Romans 8:28*

If there's one thing life has taught me, it's that "every season" really means *every* season—not just the pretty, Instagram-worthy ones.

The mountaintop moments are easy to see purpose in—the promotions, the answered prayers, the breakthroughs that make you want to do a little praise dance in your kitchen. But the valley seasons? The ones that feel confusing, heavy, or heartbreakingly unfair? Those are the ones that test whether you really believe God's still weaving purpose through it all.

I've walked through some of those seasons—seasons of loss, of waiting, of wondering if maybe God accidentally skipped over my plan while working on someone else's. But when I look back, I can see His fingerprints all over it. Every delay, every detour, every heartbreak somehow led me closer to Him.

It's funny how the things we think disqualify us are often the exact things God uses to define our purpose. The painful chapters that make you question your worth become the places He reminds you just how valuable you are.

When I was in the middle of my hardest seasons, I didn't feel valuable. I felt broken, tired, and unsure of who I even was anymore. But God doesn't measure worth the way the world does—not by productivity, success, or whether we're holding it all together. He measures it by His love. And that never changes, no matter what season we're standing in.

The truth is, your purpose isn't lost. It's not on pause. It just sometimes looks different than you expected. Maybe it's hidden in your healing. Maybe it's being refined in your waiting. Maybe it's growing quietly beneath the surface while you're convinced nothing's happening at all.

But even when you can't see it, God's still working. He's stitching every joy and every tear, every failure and every comeback, into something good—something that shows His glory and reminds you of your infinite value in Him.

So if this season feels uncertain, remember this: He's not finished. And not a single moment has been wasted.

Prayer:

Lord, thank You that every season, the beautiful and the broken, has purpose in Your plan. Help me trust that You're working for my good even when I can't see it. Remind me that my worth isn't defined by what I do, but by who I am in You. Amen.

DAY 88

His Promise, Your Peace

"In this world you will have trouble. But take heart!
I have overcome the world." — *John 16:33*

Let's be honest, I wish this verse said, "In this world you *might* have trouble," or better yet, "You'll probably *avoid* it altogether if you love Jesus enough." But no, He went ahead and made it plain: *You will have trouble.*

Well, isn't that comforting?

But here's the thing, the promise doesn't end there. Jesus didn't stop with the trouble part. He immediately followed it up with, *"Take heart! I have overcome the world."* Trouble might be guaranteed, but so is *triumph*.

I've walked through plenty of seasons that didn't feel like victory. Ones where peace felt impossible, where fear and exhaustion tried to move in rent-free. But over and over again, when I finally stopped trying to "power through" in my own strength and started resting in His promise, peace showed up. Not the kind of peace that removes the storm, the kind that steadies you in the middle of it.

That's the beauty of life with Jesus: We don't fight *for* victory—we fight *from* it. The battle's already been won. And if you belong to Him, so have you.

But here's where our worth comes in. You see, peace doesn't come from having it all together—it comes from knowing you're held together. It's remembering that your value isn't determined by your victories or your failures, but by the One who already conquered both.

The world will try to tell you that peace is found in control—in fixing, planning, and perfecting. (Guilty as charged.) But Jesus says peace is found in surrender—in trusting that even when life feels out of control, He's not.

So today, whatever you're facing, the unanswered prayers, the quiet heartbreaks, the unknowns that keep you up at night—take heart. You are already loved. Already redeemed. Already victorious.

And that's the kind of peace no trouble can touch.

> *Prayer:*
> *Jesus, thank You for being my peace when life feels chaotic. Help me live from victory, not for it. Remind me that my worth isn't shaken by the trouble around me, because You've already overcome it all. Amen.*

DAY 89

The Promise of Forever Love

"God has said, I will never leave you; never will I forsake you" — Hebrews 13:5

If you've been with me through this whole journey (and bless you if you have), then you know every single promise we've talked about—every ounce of purpose, every piece of peace, every season of waiting and wondering—it all comes back to one thing: *His love.*

That's it. The constant. The anchor. The why behind every what.

We've spent these pages unpacking what it means to live loved—to know that we're seen, chosen, called, forgiven, and free. But if I could leave you with just one truth to carry forever, it would be this: **Nothing—absolutely nothing—can separate you from His love.**

Not your past. Not your doubts. Not your mistakes. Not the voice that sometimes tells you you're too much or not enough.

Not the highs or the heartbreaks, the failures or the fears.

You could run full-speed in the wrong direction, and His love would still outrun you.

And that's what makes your worth *infinite*. Because His love doesn't waver based on your performance—it's steady because it's rooted in *who He is,* not what you do.

I think about all the times I've messed it up—the doubts I've had, the sin I've sat in, the resistance to His calling—and I still can't outrun His grace. He just keeps showing up. Over and over again. Because that's what love does.

Friend, you were worth the cross.

You were worth the pursuit.

You were worth every single promise He made.

And when this life feels too heavy or too hard or too confusing, come back to this truth: **You are loved with a forever kind of love.** The kind that doesn't fade when you fail. The kind that doesn't quit when you question. The kind that's already written the end of your story—and it's good.

Because His love never changes. Never fades. And never lets go.

> *Prayer:*
> *Lord, thank You for loving me with a love that never ends—one that holds me steady when everything else shifts. Help me live from the confidence of being fully known and fully loved. Let every promise I've learned remind me of this one truth: Nothing can separate me from You. Amen.*

DAY 90

The Promise of Forever

"I go to prepare a place for you ... that you
also may be where I am." — *John 14:2–3*

Well friend, here we are—Day 90. Ninety days of diving deep, wrestling through fear, laughing at our messiness, and reminding ourselves that we are *infinitely valued* by a God who keeps every single promise.

And this one—the *forever* promise—is the one that ties it all together.

Every "why," every "how," every "not yet" moment you've lived through leads to this truth: This world isn't the end of the story. It's just the prologue.

Jesus Himself said He's gone ahead to prepare a place for us—not a metaphorical Airbnb or a weekend getaway kind of place, but a forever home. One that doesn't crumble, fade, or require a renovation plan. (The builder in me appreciates that kind of craftsmanship, by the way.)

Knowing that our forever is secure changes how we live today. It loosens our grip on control, quiets our striving, and steadies our hearts in seasons that don't make sense. Because when you know how the story ends, you stop fearing the middle chapters.

And the best part? The same love that will welcome us home one day is the love that's been carrying us all along—through every heartbreak, every victory, every "What now, God?" moment. His love doesn't wait until heaven to show up; it's right here, right now, renewing us, redeeming us, and reminding us that we belong to Him.

So as we close these 90 days together, I want you to remember this: You are loved. Not the "sometimes," "when you get it right," "when you feel worthy" kind of love but the forever kind. The kind that builds, restores, forgives, and never lets go.

You are living proof of His promise—walking evidence of His goodness.

You are chosen.

You are called.

And you are *already home* in His heart.

So take a deep breath, my brave friend. Keep stepping boldly into the life He's written for you—one promise, one prayer, one brave act of faith at a time.

Because forever starts here.

> *Prayer:*
> Lord, thank You for every promise You've spoken and every one You've already fulfilled. Thank You that my forever is secure in You. Help me live bravely, love deeply, and walk fully in the truth that I am infinitely loved, chosen, and worth every ounce of Your grace. Amen.

To The Extraordinary Woman Reading This:

If you made it this far—all ninety days of reflection, tears, laughter, conviction, and grace—I want you to know something: I am so dang proud of you.

This devotional wasn't written from a mountaintop moment or some perfectly curated spiritual highlight reel. It was written from the middle—the messy, unfiltered, "God, are You sure about this?" middle. The place where fear still creeps in, where faith sometimes feels small, and where I've had to learn, again and again, that *He meets me right where I am.*

And friend, that's the calling on my life—to meet *you* right where *you* are.

Maybe you're the woman who cusses a little, who pours herself a glass of wine, or two, and wonders if that disqualifies her from being used by God. Maybe you love Jesus but still lose your patience in traffic. Maybe you've walked through heartache, shame, exhaustion, or doubt and questioned whether you're too much of a mess to be meaningful.

This was written for *you.*

Because I've been her too. The overachiever trying to earn love that was already given. The brave expert who only got that title because she spent so long living in fear. The woman who's wrestled with her calling, questioned her worth, and had to remind herself daily that "not enough" was never part of God's vocabulary.

But this is what I've learned:

Our *Who* is found in Him.

Our *Why* is anchored in His plan and purpose.

And our *How*—well, that's where brave comes in.

Because brave doesn't mean fearless. It means you feel the fear and take the step anyway—trusting that even when you stumble, He's still steady beneath your feet.

Over these ninety days, we've explored His love, His plan, and His promise—and how every one of them points back to your infinite value in Christ. His love is what makes you worthy. His plan is what gives your life purpose. And His promise? It's the proof that He's not done with you yet.

So if you're still figuring it out, still healing, still fighting through the noise of self-doubt—that's okay. You don't have to have it all together. You just have to have your heart open. Because God isn't looking for perfection; He's looking for presence.

And the same God who met me in my mess—the one who turned fear into brave, resistance into surrender, and striving into peace—will meet you in yours.

So keep going, beautiful friend.

Keep showing up, even when it's hard.

Keep trusting that every chapter—even the ones that feel like rubble—is part of a redemptive story being written by a God who adores you.

You were created on purpose, for a purpose.

You are loved without condition, guided with intention, and kept by promises that never fail.

And above all, you are infinitely valued—not for what you do, but because of *Whose* you are.

Now go live it.

Be brave.

And remember: You ARE more than less than.

Amy Druhot

Acknowledgments

On my journey of faith, God placed remarkable women along my path—each one gifting me something unique, something holy, something I didn't know I needed until it shaped me. Scripture reminds us in *Proverbs 27:17* that "iron sharpens iron," and in *Hebrews 12:1* that we are surrounded by "a great cloud of witnesses." These women have been exactly that for me—sharpening, strengthening, surrounding, and steadying me as I grew into the woman God was calling me to be.

Linda Guyton—*Psalm 40:3*—As a little girl she taught me what it meant to carry a song from God in my heart.

Pat Thrasher—*Romans 12:13*—Hospitality in its purest form. The kind of welcome that feels like Jesus at the door.

Julie Lindeman—*1 Corinthians 15:58*—A living example of steadfastness. Faith that does not move, bend, or bow.

Marilyn Liles—*Micah 6:8*—Humility and acceptance in motion. She lives grace with such quiet strength.

Becky Davis—*Proverbs 17:17*—My childhood best friend who taught me the value of loyal, lasting, shared faith, friendship.

Lisa Apking—*Matthew 7:25*—My foundation-setter. She showed me what faith built on the Rock truly looks like.

Phyllis Sawyer—*1 Peter 3:4*—Beauty without self-centeredness. A gentle spirit with eternal worth. And the church where I answered the altar call that changed my life.

Kara Handy & Dawn Thurber—*Ecclesiastes 4:9–10*—Teen friendships rooted in Christ. Proof that God plants purpose even in our youth. (They also probably kept me out of more trouble than I'd like to know)

Sharon Heym—*Proverbs 31:25*—A radiant spirit of joy, fun, and freedom. She reminded me not to care so much about what others think.

Carolyn Wheeling—*Proverbs 16:31*—Wisdom and mature faith lived out with authenticity.

Shannon Amerson—*Jeremiah 29:11*—She saw God's future plans for me long before I saw them myself.

Caroline Kalentzos—*Joshua 1:9*—Confidence in calling. She encouraged me to step boldly into what God was shaping.

Melissa Taft—*1 Samuel 16:7*—She saw my heart and the calling inside me and spoke it over me before I could even name it.

Sarah Keeble—*James 5:16*
My spiritual sister and prayer warrior—you've covered me in intercession more times than I can count.

Hope Londeree—*1 Corinthians 12:4-6*
For being the one who made me see ministry differently—not as a stage or a title, but as a way of living that shines His love.

Mary Druhot, my MIL—*1 John 3:18*
For teaching me selfless love—not by words, but by the way she lives it daily.

And for **every woman not named here but woven into my** story—I carry pieces of each of you. God used you as mirrors, mentors, motivators, and ministers in ways you may never fully know.

Finally—and most tenderly—**my mom**.

She was the root of my faith. She introduced me to Jesus, placed Scripture in my hands, and made sure I memorized verses long before I understood how deeply I'd need them. *Proverbs 22:6* says, "Train up a child in the way they should go, and when they are old, they will not depart from it."

Mom, that is your legacy in me. Thank you.

To all of you—thank you for being part of the "good work" God began in me. This devotional is not just my story… it is the echo of every woman who ever spoke life, truth, courage, and Christ into my journey.

About the Author

Amy Druhot is a speaker, author, and faith-led leadership mentor known for her authentic storytelling, practical wisdom, and signature message of brave, Christ-centered living. As the founder of **Just Brave It,** she equips women across industries to lead with courage, clarity, and Kingdom purpose—even in the most secular spaces.

A TEDx speaker and award-winning sales executive with over two decades in the homebuilding industry, Amy has built a reputation for inspiring rooms, shifting cultures, and empowering women to embrace their calling with confidence. Her work has been featured at national conferences, leadership summits, and industry events, where her blend of humor, transparency, and biblical truth consistently resonates with audiences.

Amy is the best-selling author of *Just Brave It* and a mentor to women who desire to lead like Jesus in a modern world. Her mission is simple: to meet women right in the middle of their beautifully messy lives and point them toward the God who loves them, calls them, equips them, and never lets them go.

She lives in Midlothian, Virginia, with her husband and their blended family, where she continues writing, speaking, and bravely following the purpose God planted in her.

Learn more at **www.justbraveit.com.**